D0470358

Praise for
The Babylon Bee Guide to Wokeness

"The Babylon Bee is the funniest site on social media next to my stuff, and this book hits wokeness with a truthful comedy sledgehammer right between its pronouns. Wokeness is so outrageously ridiculous that The Bee actually gets fact-checked because the woke are literally a parody of they/themselves. This book is flat-out hilarious and sadly true. But enough about The Bee—check my site for tour dates."

—Larry the Cable Guy, comedian, actor, and recording artist

"If you're looking for a careful academic analysis of the philosophical underpinnings of the First Amendment, this book is not for you. But if you're looking to laugh your ass off while The Bee slays the Left's sacred cows, look no further! Satire always beats idiocy, and this book annihilates the woke shibboleths of the modern age."

—Ted Cruz, United States senator from Texas

"Many books are chosen, but few are called amazing. If you're estrogen-challenged, then read *The Babylon Bee Guide to Wokeness* and a man-bun will sprout from your head. It's like *The Bell Jar* in that it's funnier than The Onion."

—Doug TenNapel, bitter YouTuber and creator of Earthworm Jim

"The Babylon Bee is by far the funniest outlet in America. And their new book is the funniest new book in America. Which isn't saying a lot, since they're in competition with people like Stephen Colbert."

—Ben Shapiro, political commentator, author, and cofounder of The Daily Wire

"When you consider our culture today, you either have to laugh uproariously or repeatedly smack yourself in the forehead with a hatchet. This book will make you laugh uproariously and costs about the same as a decent hatchet. So your call."

—**Andrew Klavan,** bestselling novelist and host of *The Andrew Klavan Show*

"At times the woke crowd does and says things that make me think, 'Surely this is satire.' Unfortunately, it isn't. The woke/anti-racist movement has now gone so far that satirizing it has become difficult. Thankfully, The Babylon Bee is so adept at satire that it is able to pull it off even in this treacherous territory. With mockery that rivals that of Elijah before the prophets of Baal, this book takes on the pernicious ideology eating away at the core of all we hold dear and exposes its most ridiculous tenets, all while reminding the reader that sometimes we just need to laugh—even if it's only to keep from crying."

—**Voddie Baucham Jr.,** dean of the School of Divinity at African Christian University in Lusaka, Zambia, and author of the bestseller *Fault Lines*

"This is the satirical skewering of wokeness the world needs. The cultural commentary is razor-precise, unrelentingly funny, and air-clearing. In the spirit of Luther, Lewis, and other eminently cancellable cisgender patriarchalist oppressors whose names we shall soon biomechanically erase from our minds, *The Babylon Bee Guide to Wokeness* tells the truth and mocks the devil."

—**Dr. Owen Strachan,** provost of Grace Bible Theological Seminary and author of *Christianity and Wokeness*

"Until I read *The Babylon Bee Guide to Wokeness*, I had no sympathy for headless treesexual elves who ride unicycles. But I woke up to their existence and realize both my privilege and how utterly insane wokeness is. Five stars, mostly because of the pictures."

—**Erick Erickson,** blogger and host of *Atlanta's Evening News with Erick Erickson*

"I am a gay man, and therefore, as you will learn from reading this book, you have to do what I say. Plus it's hilarious and you'll love it. Buy it and read it, bigot!"

—**Spencer Klavan,** host of the *Young Heretics* podcast

"The Babylon Bee is more savage than I am, and Kyle Mann has effortlessly trolled me on Twitter like no one else. I heartily endorse this book—especially the part about burning it all to the ground."

    —Michael Malice, author, columnist, and host of the *YOUR WELCOME* podcast

"Finally, a book that can make us all exactly the same! How great will it be when no one has a different opinion?! Read this book so you too can 'peacefully' burn down entire city blocks, shout the fascists down so they can no longer speak, show your 'whitey, honky, Jethro-sister-marrying' redneck how offensive they can be when they name-call and stereotype…racists. The Babylon Bee has finally written a humor book making fun of those who are humorless. Hilarious on so many levels."

    —Glenn Beck, founder of TheBlaze.com, bestselling author, and nationally syndicated
        radio host

"Laughter is the best medicine in our current toxic world, and The Babylon Bee is always good for fun. I love the lampoons they do of me. Their work reminds us all not to take ourselves so freaking seriously."

    —Dave Ramsey, bestselling author and radio host

The Babylon Bee Guide to Wokeness

The Babylon Bee Guide to

WOKENESS

How to Take Your Wokeness to the Next Level by Canceling Friends, Breaking Windows, and Burning It All to the Ground

SALEM
BOOKS

an imprint of Regnery Publishing
Washington, D.C.

Copyright © 2021 by The Babylon Bee

All rights reserved. No part of this publication may be reproduced or transmitted in any form or by any means electronic or mechanical, including photocopy, recording, or any information storage and retrieval system now known or to be invented, without permission in writing from the publisher, except by a reviewer who wishes to quote brief passages in connection with a review written for inclusion in a magazine, newspaper, website, or broadcast.

Salem Books™ is a trademark of Salem Communications Holding Corporation
Regnery® is a registered trademark and its colophon is a trademark of Salem Communications Holding Corporation

Cataloging-in-Publication data on file with the Library of Congress

ISBN: 978-1-68451-271-3
eISBN: 978-1-68451-272-0

Published in the United States by
Salem Books
An Imprint of Regnery Publishing
A Division of Salem Media Group
Washington, D.C.
www.SalemBooks.com

Manufactured in the United States of America
10 9 8 7 6 5 4 3 2

Books are available in quantity for promotional or premium use.
For information on discounts and terms, please visit our website: www.SalemBooks.com

This book is dedicated to
Joseph Stalin, a woke hero
and champion of the
oppressed proletariat.

*"Get woke or get a 7.62 round
to the face lol."*
—*Joe*

Contents

Introduction

Welcome to the

Woke Zone

Greetings, comrade! You've picked up this book because you want to be woke. And we at The Babylon Bee are the enlightened sages of this great new religion of wokeness. We're ready to guide you on the path to enlightenment—if you're ready to join us on this journey.

What is being woke, anyway, you might ask? "Woke" is a term you hear thrown around all the time, usually by backward Republicans who are trying to make fun of people like us who care about social justice.

Being woke means **waking up to the cause**. What cause? Every far-left, radical, communist, Marxist cause we can think of. The entire agenda of the Left.

BEING WOKE MEANS:

Wokeness isn't a private religion you can keep to yourself. Once you see the world through woke eyes, you'll never be the same, and you'll never be able to stop telling your friends about your new beliefs. Kind of like when you join CrossFit or become vegan—or get an air fryer.

BEING WOKE MEANS:

Realizing the problems in your life are not your fault

In fact, when you really think about it, nothing is your fault. Blame everyone else for your problems. This is the first step to being woke.

Finding your identity not in objective reality, but in your feelings

In the past, people would find their identities in objective truths, like biology, their family, and philosophy. But woke people know better: they simply choose a subjective identity that makes them feel good.

Worshiping the planet because humanity is evil

You can't truly be an advocate for Mother Earth until you recognize that humanity is always the bad guy. Fight hard for population control, which of course never includes you or anyone you like.

Rejecting organized religion and mindlessly believing the Left

It's important to get rid of outdated ideas like doctrine and moral values and instead believe whatever the people on the Left tell you.

Finding the racism, sexism, and hatred in everything

They're everywhere—and you can see them if you try hard and believe in yourself.

Changing your profile picture to match the current fad

Black squares? Check. Rainbow profile overlays? Check. Save Harambe? We can all agree on that one.

Brainwashing your kids to hate life and be miserable

Because you don't want to raise a generation of happy, well-adjusted kids—that's what NAZIS do.

Rioting

—sorry, peacefully protesting—in the name of justice.

Never, ever being satisfied and having happiness, but instead constantly complaining about everything

Doesn't this sound great? Rather than eking out some kind of meaning and satisfaction in your life, you get to constantly complain as though you are still a three-year-old. Hooray!

Becoming an absolutely horrible person to be around

You'll know you've truly arrived at a state of wokeness once everyone in your life—even your kids, your parents, your closest friends, and your pets—no longer want to be around you because you're a real stick in the mud. Success!

Sounds great, doesn't it? It sure is. Being woke is a journey without end. You'll never truly arrive—you'll simply have to strive to **do better** for the rest of your life.

We'll explore each of these areas of being woke throughout this handy guide. You'll want to carry this with you on your college campus, at your home, and at your church so you can make sure you turn everyone around you into the wokest version of themselves they possibly can be.

Wokeness touches every part of life. Once you're woke, you won't be able to see anything the same way again. You won't be able to have a normal, friendly interaction with anyone without noticing all the **microaggressions** they're casually lobbing in your direction like miniature, incredibly hurtful hand grenades.

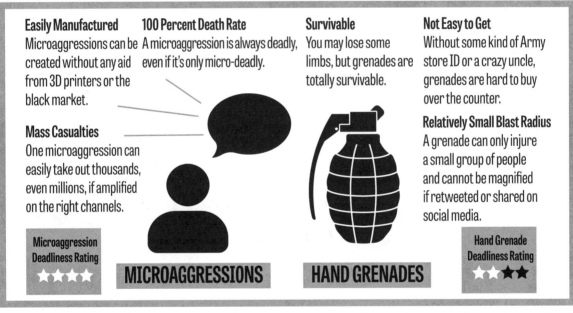

Microaggressions vs. hand grenades: Which are deadlier?

Easily Manufactured
Microaggressions can be created without any aid from 3D printers or the black market.

Mass Casualties
One microaggression can easily take out thousands, even millions, if amplified on the right channels.

100 Percent Death Rate
A microaggression is always deadly, even if it's only micro-deadly.

Survivable
You may lose some limbs, but grenades are totally survivable.

Not Easy to Get
Without some kind of Army store ID or a crazy uncle, grenades are hard to buy over the counter.

Relatively Small Blast Radius
A grenade can only injure a small group of people and cannot be magnified if retweeted or shared on social media.

Microaggression Deadliness Rating ★★★★

MICROAGGRESSIONS

HAND GRENADES

Hand Grenade Deadliness Rating ★★★★

It's a good thing you're joining us on this journey, because those who get woke are immediately placed in a magical category called "the right side of history." You don't want to be on the wrong side of history, do you? We didn't think so. A lot of people have ended up on the wrong side of history, like people who hate *The Last Jedi* and people who bought into HD DVD instead of Blu-ray.

While it's true you're a terrible person, you still have a small spark of something good in you because you decided it was time to get woke.

So we're going to begin this journey together right now.

YOUR WOKE JOURNEY

The journey to wokeness is full of twists, turns, and detours. This road map depicts some of the ways one can go astray on the path to wokeness. Can you make it to the finish line without getting red-pilled?

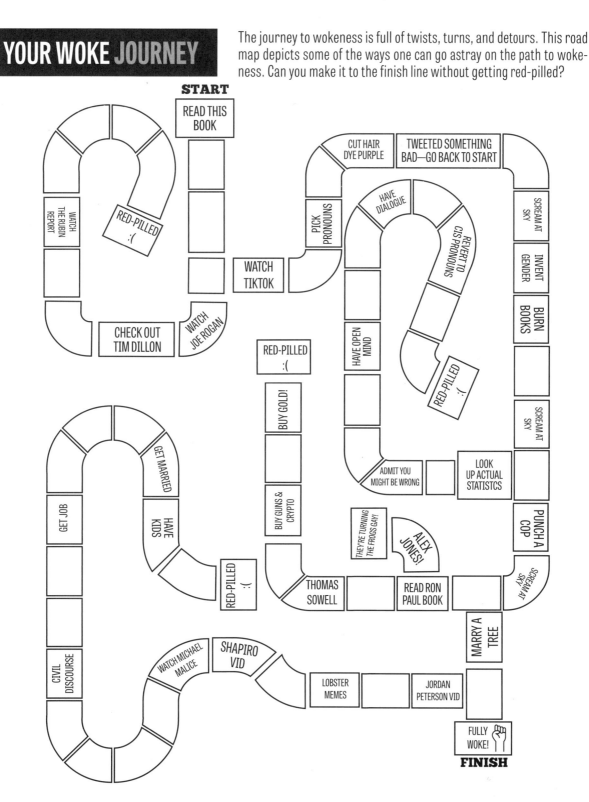

YOU ARE A RACIST

Let's start things out here by getting one important thing out of the way:

You are a racist, misogynist, patriarchal, and bigoted oppressor. Scientists have been able to locate the many hate centers of the human body; they divide broadly according to the diagram below (Figure A).

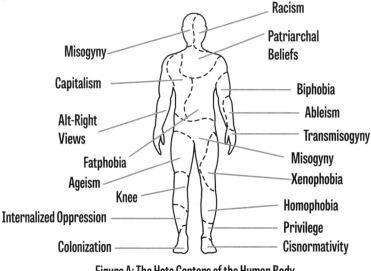

Misogyny

Capitalism

Alt-Right Views

Fatphobia

Ageism

Knee

Internalized Oppression

Colonization

Racism

Patriarchal Beliefs

Biphobia

Ableism

Transmisogyny

Misogyny

Xenophobia

Homophobia

Privilege

Cisnormativity

Figure A: The Hate Centers of the Human Body

Now, you're not as bad as some people. You're probably not literally Hitler, though it would be wise to get a DNA test just to make sure. And if you are Hitler, you're probably reading this on an e-book, because, you know, the paper version of this book is quite flammable. Well, tablets are too, but I bet they have a higher melting point, and Hitler could probably get at least this far before the whole thing turned into molten glass and silicon.

Anyway. You're not Hitler (probably). But you're still bad and racist.

You might be thinking to yourself, "Hey, that's pretty offensive. You don't even know me. I'm not a racist."

If you're thinking that, well, we've got you right where we want you.

Because **that's exactly what a bigoted, oppressive, and privileged racist would say.**

Yep. If you say you're not a racist, you're only proving that you are a racist. This is the way of the woke.

Experts recommend getting a DNA test to make sure you are not literally Hitler.

THINGS RACISTS SAY

- "I love your hair!"
- "Where are you from?"
- "Did your parents grow up here?"
- "Can you make good kimchi?"
- "How do you pronounce that?"
- "Are you good at basketball?"
- "I like your name!"
- "I don't always think about race."

- "I appreciate your culture."
- "I do not appreciate your culture."
- "I'll be friends with anyone."
- "Yeeeeehaw!!!"
- "America is an alright place."
- "Y'all" or "Bless her heart!"
- "Watch this Ben Shapiro video."
- "I know some OK white people."

Now, you might then think, "OK, then I AM a racist, which makes me NOT racist." Nope. Not the way this works. If you think you're a racist, then you're also a racist. You're now a double racist, because you just admitted it. Not good!

$$\frac{Privilege^2 + Gender^3}{\sqrt{Race}} = \sqrt{\frac{(Age^3 - Weight)(Skin\ Color^2 + Income)^3}{\sqrt{Thinking\ you\ are\ not\ racist}}} = \text{DOUBLE RACISM}$$

But don't worry: there's always hope. You can try really, really hard to do better. And as long as you have never made a mistake in your life, tweeted anything dumb, or done anything that we even slightly disagree with, you just might get along great.

And you've already taken the first step on your path to redemption, because you've purchased this book for full MSRP. Every dollar will be counted toward your salvation. (If you bought this book at a discount, repent. Educate yourself. Do better. Buy five more copies as reparations.)

THINGS THIS BOOK WILL TEACH YOU

This guide will teach you many useful and important things, such as the following:

You'll learn all this and more with our handy guide.

Will this absolve you of your sins? Of course not. Once you've achieved the revered status of "woke," you'll have to continue to try hard to do better. There is no final salvation here like in those backward religions of ages past. Instead, if you make the tiniest mistake, it's back to the bottom of the ladder for you. You'll have to educate yourself, make space for more oppressed voices to lecture you on your internalized and toxically problematic views, and do better and better and better.

So buckle up, comrade. We're getting woke.

Chapter 1
Intersectionality and
Identity

Let's get started, class. Check your privilege at the door, because it's time for you to learn about intersectionality.

We know it sounds like a made-up word, and that's because it is. We just made it up, like, a few years ago, because the races and classes were starting to get along and we needed something to break up all that peace and harmony and introduce some good, old-fashioned, Marxist class warfare.

Intersectionality is a concept wherein you can add oppression points to yourself for every oppressed identity you can even remotely identify with. Even if it's a stretch. The game, then, here in Wokeland is to find as many of these identities as possible and apply these labels to yourself so you can feel righteous—and so you can get more money from the government and blame everyone else for your problems.

In olden times, like back in 2009, if you had problems in your life, you'd think hard about the choices that led you to that low point. Then you'd change your approach to life. Maybe you'd change your worldview, or go get a new job, or work harder. You'd apologize to other people for the way you'd behaved. Then you'd dust yourself off and go out into the cold, unforgiving world and give it another go.

This approach is **decidedly not woke**.

It's important to remember that **your problems are not your fault**. They are the fault of the oppressor class. Your parents? Oppressors. Your teachers? Oppressors. People with a different skin color than you? Oppressors. Anyone who disagrees with your woke worldview? You guessed it. Oppressors.

IDENTIFYING OPPRESSORS IN YOUR LIFE

Your neighbors

Your boss

White people

Your parents

Elon Musk

Amazon

Your babysitter

That guy who cut you off in traffic

Everyone who has it better than you

THE INTERSECTIONALITY MATRIX

Humans are varied. Some are old, some are fat, some are from Kentucky, and others are from Kenya. Some can touch the tip of their nose with their tongue, and others can flatulate on command. We all have intersections of privileges and disadvantages. The point is not to see each of us as unique individuals, but to parse all of humanity into groups based on these obscure and often meaningless attributes so that a new minority group can be created.

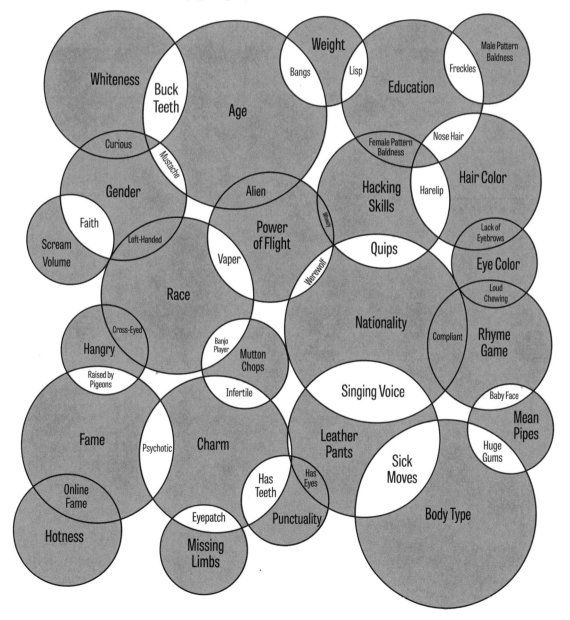

So, to solve the problem of who's an innocent victim and who's a perpetrator of evil white supremacy, we came up with the intersectionality matrix. You want to land on as many intersections of oppression as possible.

Here are just a few examples of some oppressed identities you can select:

OPPRESSION IDENTIFIER

To create your own oppressed class, simply follow the instructions to combine an option from each list and immediately identify as that.

DISABILITY	GENDER	RACE/CREED	BONUS
(1st Letter of First Name)	(3rd Letter of Middle Name)	(2nd Letter of Last Name)	(Last Letter of First Name)
A. Underdeveloped	A. Cisgendered	A. Pacific Islander	A. With Nine Kids
B. Anxious	B. Bisexual	B. New Jerseyan	B. On a Boat
C. Bipedal	C. Bipolar	C. White	C. Currently on Fire
D. One-Legged	D. Pansexual	D. Hmong	D. With Honey Glaze
E. Huge-Gummed	E. Trans-Siberian	E. Arab	E. From Space
F. Balding	F. Agender	F. Indigenous	F. With a Slice of Lime
G. Obese	G. Androgynous	G. African American	G. With No Parents
H. Deaf	H. Transsexual	H. Armenian	H. With Bear Lungs
I. Blind	I. Demigender	I. Calvinist	I. On the Rocks
J. Hirsute	J. Feminine Adjacent	J. Kyrgyz	J. Without Any Rhythm
K. Headless	K. Gender Apathetic	K. Uyghur	K. Who Died Years Ago
L. Many-Fingered	L. Treesexual	L. Muslim	L. In a Body Cast
M. Kneeless	M. Gender-Neutral	M. Christian	M. Who Sucks at Tetris
N. Boneless	N. Gender-Fluid	N. Alaskan	N. Who Can't Spell for Crap
O. Squeaky-Breathing	O. Gender-Nonconforming	O. Eskimo	O. With No Sense of Smell
P. Buck-Toothed	P. Graygender	P. Elf	P. Who Fell Down a Well
Q. Harelipped	Q. Hermaphroditic	Q. Haitian	Q. Who Eats Babies
R. Crazy-Eyed	R. Multigender	R. Quaker	R. On Stilts
S. Cyclopian	S. Omnigender	S. Simpson	S. On Top of Old Smoky
T. Double Amputee	T. Polygender	T. Troglodyte	T. On a Unicycle
U. Legally Blonde	U. Math-Loving	U. Philistine	U. Who Sucks at Harmonies
V. Papier-Mâché	V. Cat-Loving	V. Fishmonger	V. With Large Moles
W. Flea-Ridden	W. Germophobe	W. Lunatic	W. On Their Death Bed
X. Horse-Faced	X. Homophobe	X. Turkish	X. With No Spleen
Y. Jawless	Y. Stone Butch	Y. Tater Tot	Y. Created by Mad Scientists
Z. Pointy-Headed	Z. Trigender	Z. Amazonian	Z. Built by Jim Henson

EXAMPLES OF OPPRESSED CLASSES

Still not quite sure how this all works? That's OK. You're new at this. We're going to give you some examples of oppressed intersectional classes you can choose from. Just remember that you can be any oppressed identity you want, as long as you try hard and believe in yourself.

Remember how Elsa in *Frozen* didn't listen to her family and friends and just decided to BE HERSELF? That's what you need to do: just let it go. Sure, Elsa almost mass-murdered her entire kingdom by covering it with an ice storm and nearly stabbed her sister in the heart with an icicle, but hey! She was LIVING HER TRUTH.

Or remember how Ariel didn't listen to her dad—a mean, patriarchal ruler who wanted her to be oppressed as a wealthy, influential mermaid princess for the rest of her life? Yes, she almost got herself and her entire kingdom turned into those little weird goblin things growing in the Sea Witch's lair, and her dad and the prince had to come rescue her, but still! She wasn't going to listen to any mean old patriarch!

You need to be just like these Disney princesses. Live your truth. Be like one of these stunning and brave heroes of oppression:

HEROES OF OPPRESSION Your heart will bleed for each of these brave lads and lasses—not to mention lxsses—who suffer at the hands of the patriarchy.

Obese Cat-Loving Eskimo in a Body Cast

Headless Treesexual Elf on a Unicycle

Buck-Toothed Trans Calvinist on Stilts

One-Legged Lesbian Arab from Space

Blind Math-Loving Philistine Who Died Years Ago

Many-Fingered Germophobic Quaker with Moles

Intersectionality

Take a look at our handy chart here in order to place yourself on the intersectional oppression matrix so you know just how bad you have it in life:

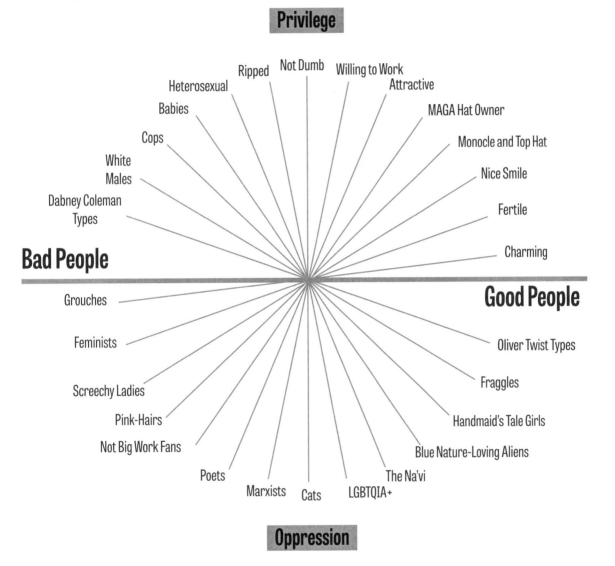

Privilege

Ripped · Not Dumb · Willing to Work
Heterosexual · Attractive
Babies · MAGA Hat Owner
Cops · Monocle and Top Hat
White Males · Nice Smile
Dabney Coleman Types · Fertile
Charming

Bad People — **Good People**

Grouches
Feminists · Oliver Twist Types
Screechy Ladies · Fraggles
Pink-Hairs · Handmaid's Tale Girls
Not Big Work Fans · Blue Nature-Loving Aliens
Poets · The Na'vi
Marxists · Cats · LGBTQIA+

Oppression

No matter what identity you select, the important thing is that you never, ever take responsibility for problems in your own life. In short, go out and criticize the world before you clean your room—because your dirty room is everyone else's fault.

Let's take a closer look at each axis of your identity.

GENDER

Gender is an extremely important aspect of your identity.

There are many genders you can choose from, including cisgender, bigender, gender neutral, and super-double-omni-sexual-nonbinding-gender-non-hippopotamus. (For more, see our chapter on Gender.)

Remember: gender is both entirely made up and imaginary, and it also cannot be contradicted by anyone else. It is eternal, set in stone, never changing, an immutable part of who you are.

Until you change it. Because you can change it at any time. And we encourage you to do exactly that whenever you find a gender identity that helps you climb the intersectional ladder. Maybe you once declared yourself as agender, and now millions of people say they are agender. It's just not cool anymore. It just doesn't give you the woke points that it used to. So change it! Declare you are a gender-fluid-dragonkin-transgender-semi-grey ace with an Enneagram wing nine. Now, no one else is like you—well, until everyone copies you and you have to go and change it again.

With gender, always stay one step ahead of everyone else. And remember, it's like going to a buffet in Vegas: take a little bit of everything and just have fun with it!

RACE

OK, so, things might get a little confusing here. Because while you can change your gender at the drop of a hat, race is immutable. You can just identify as the other sex or another gender at any time, but don't try this with race because you'll get eaten alive. While biological sex is a myth, biological races are set in stone.

So, how do you get a leg up on everyone else when you can't change your race? Well, there are a few approaches.

First, you can search deep in your family history for a great-great-great-great-step-uncle who might have had 1/64th Native American blood. Then, you can use that to get admitted to a good college and get some great scholarships.

Next, if you are white, you can kind of make up for it a little bit by constantly tweeting about how terrible white people are. The truly oppressed woke people of color will never entirely forgive you for being white, of course, but you can start chipping away at that debt little by little. Here are a few tweets for you to try on for size.

TWEETS FOR WHITE PEOPLE TO SOUND LESS RACIST

Melanie J @melanie4justice81

UGH WHITE PEOPLE

9:09 PM - May 3, 2020

Melanie J @melanie4justice81

THOSE WHITES ARE AT IT AGAIN.

9:09 PM - May 3, 2020

Melanie J @melanie4justice81

KILL · ALL · WHITE · PEOPLE ·

9:09 PM - May 3, 2020

Melanie J @melanie4justice81

DON'T LISTEN TO ANY WHITE PEOPLE (WELL EXCEPT ME OF COURSE)

9:09 PM - May 3, 2020

Melanie J @melanie4justice81

I AM SORRY ON BEHALF OF WHITE PEOPLE

9:09 PM - May 3, 2020

Finally, the truly daring antiracists sometimes just go ahead and try a little casual blackface. Rachel Dolezal, Justin Trudeau, Ralph Northam—these are just a few of the people that went for broke in denying their whiteness by dressing up as another race. And good ol' Justin almost had us fooled!

But yeah, don't try that. It usually doesn't play out very well.

Why is it OK to identify as any gender or sexual orientation but not race? Why can you declare that you're a woman and everyone must accept it as the gospel truth, but the second you engage in a little casual blackface you get in trouble?

We're not sure. We didn't make up the rules. But we sure as heck are gonna play by them so we don't get canceled.

The main takeaway here for race is to **BE WOKE, NOT WHITE.**

CLASS

Your class is an important part of your spot on the intersectionality matrix. What is class, anyway? Class is how much money you have, how cool of a car you drive, and whether or not you have one of those fancy fridges that dispenses ice and water right from the door. Just as in all the other intersectional categories, you want everyone to know that you are the lowest possible class.

The problem, of course, is that if you're reading this book, you're probably pretty privileged.

Oh no! How do you solve this problem? By looking for class oppression in everything, deemphasizing any privilege you have, and pointing out how much better other people have it than you.

Use slogans like "Eat the Rich," even though you're one of the richest people in all of human history. If you're a hundred-thousand-aire, denounce millionaires. If you're a millionaire, denounce billionaires.

EVERYONE WHO HAS MORE THAN YOU IS WHAT'S WRONG WITH THE WORLD.

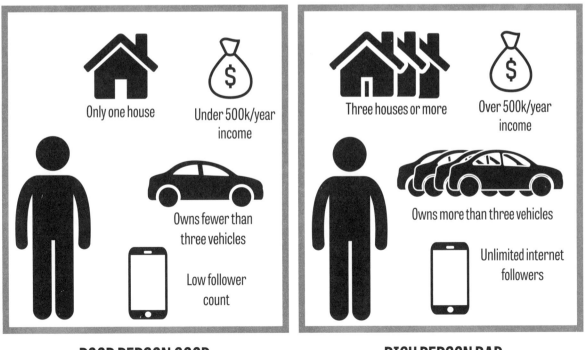

POOR PERSON GOOD   **RICH PERSON BAD**

RELIGION

This one is pretty simple: Any religion is acceptable except Christianity. Yes, we prefer if you're an atheist who simply bows to the whims of the state—but any religion that's OK with social justice is useful for us woke folks.

The main thing is that your religion must conform to every demand of wokeness. Even Christianity can be useful, after all, if you discard its main tenets in service of wokeness.

But whatever religion you pick, make sure it's an oppressed, exotic, unique belief system that can score you woke points, and not something basic and lame like Christianity. If you must be a Christian, though, because your lame parents make you go to church as long as you live under their floor or whatever, co-opt Christianity for social justice. The only good church is a woke church.

We'll teach you more about all this later, but for now, check out these cool, fun, unique, WOKE religions you can be:

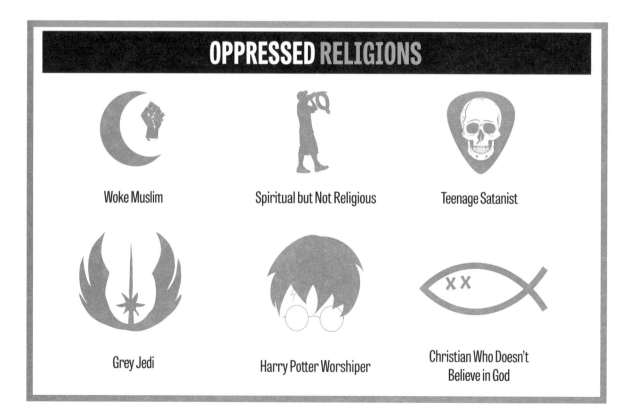

OPPRESSED RELIGIONS

Woke Muslim

Spiritual but Not Religious

Teenage Satanist

Grey Jedi

Harry Potter Worshiper

Christian Who Doesn't Believe in God

NATIONALITY

Being woke is all about diversity. We love people of ALL nationalities and want the whole world to just be a big melting pot of all cultures, creeds, and nations.

Except, of course, Americans. America is a disgusting place filled with white nationalists who could learn a thing or two from more advanced socialist countries like Venezuela or the Soviet Union.

So if you're a white Christian American male, you've got a real problem, because your entire existence is basically a plague upon the earth. You need to spend all your days online apologizing to people from superior countries for the place you're ashamed to call home. The nice thing is you don't actually have to put your money where your mouth is and move to Canada. You can just constantly threaten to leave the country and say things like "UGH, I'M SORRY FOR MY FELLOW AMERICANS" and "I'M TOTALLY MOVING TO CANADA THE NEXT TIME A REPUBLICAN WINS THE PRESIDENCY!!!" But you can keep reaping the benefits of American prosperity while never leaving for a country that's not doing as well.

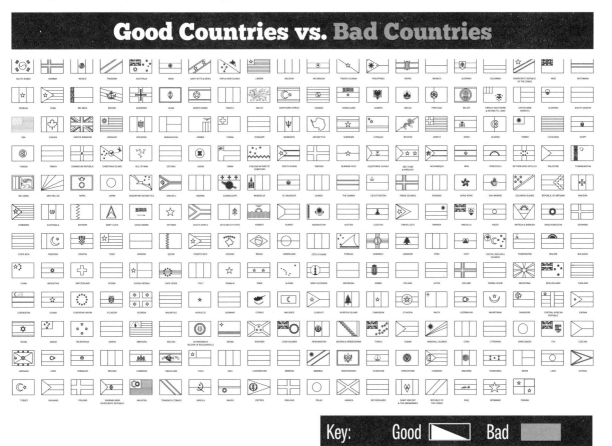

LIFE IS TOUGH SO DON'T EVEN TRY

The moral of the story when it comes to intersectionality is that life isn't fair. While previous, less-enlightened generations confronted life's fundamental inequity by stoically accepting it and trying to make life as pleasant as possible for themselves and their families in spite of their hardships, we know better.

We've become woke. We now realize that the only way to confront the countless instances of oppression and inequality in the world is to complain loudly about them and demand that other people fix our problems. Don't try hard. Don't try to create a little bit of order in this world of chaos.

Instead, whine. Loudly.

Chapter 2

Race

| Bad | Better | Best |

Race is a social construct created by white people to excuse their oppression of black and brown bodies. It's also the most important thing about you.

In short, race is nothing, yet it is everything. Don't try to make sense of it. Do you have a Ph.D.? Have you published peer-reviewed papers? Didn't think so. So sit down and learn something!

The reason race is so important is because everything in life can be explained by power imbalances between oppressors and the oppressed. Some people think life is infinitely more complicated and that humans are actually embodied souls with a will and moral conscience who can make right or wrong choices, but that's dumb—because we said so and we went to college.

We prefer instead to look at human beings as meaningless clumps of cells whose every interaction can be easily explained by a very simple materialistic theory that helps us get a ton of scholarly papers published. And if you don't agree with all our conclusions, you're a racist!

One of the most important keys to being woke is to think about race at all times. Every time you meet people, you should be thinking primarily of their skin color, because it's their single most defining characteristic. It affects all their experiences, thoughts, and beliefs. Most importantly, people's skin color will tell you whether they are oppressors or the oppressed. You can know pretty much all the most important things about people by simply looking at their skin color.

WHAT'S IMPORTANT ABOUT YOU?

Use this handy guide to determine what is really important about you, your friends, your family, even your own children.

Important	Unimportant
Race	Personality
Ethnicity	Thoughts
Nationality	Faith
Genetics	Opinion
Skin Color	Individuality
Ethnic Culture	Name
Pigment	Hopes
Melanin	Dreams
Epidermis	Desires
Top Quarter-Inch of Flesh	Screenplay Ideas
Skin Tone	Life Advice
	Favorite Kind of Ice Cream

DEFINING RACE

You might be reading this and thinking, "Huh. That seems a little racist." Well, you're wrong! We just recently changed the definition of "racist" to mean "anyone who refuses to look at someone through the lens of race." Yup, the dictionary actually let us change the definition. We were a little surprised they let us do that, but hey—we're not complaining!

You may think race is just about the level of melanin in your skin. The truth is, it's much more complicated than that. There's more to being white than white skin, and there's more to being a person of color than dark skin.

To see race from a woke perspective, you must understand that there are really only two races: white people and the oppressed. Being in one of these two groups requires more than just skin color—it requires the right attitudes and ideology.

It's important to know the difference. Here is a breakdown of the characteristics of each race:

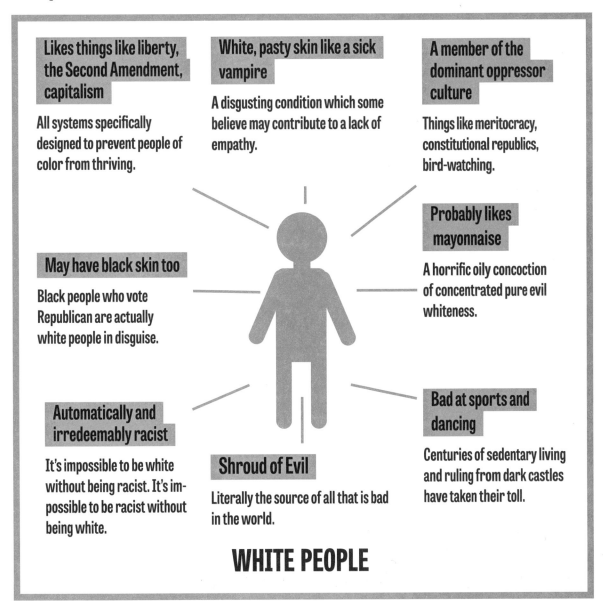

Likes things like liberty, the Second Amendment, capitalism

All systems specifically designed to prevent people of color from thriving.

White, pasty skin like a sick vampire

A disgusting condition which some believe may contribute to a lack of empathy.

A member of the dominant oppressor culture

Things like meritocracy, constitutional republics, bird-watching.

Probably likes mayonnaise

A horrific oily concoction of concentrated pure evil whiteness.

May have black skin too

Black people who vote Republican are actually white people in disguise.

Automatically and irredeemably racist

It's impossible to be white without being racist. It's impossible to be racist without being white.

Shroud of Evil

Literally the source of all that is bad in the world.

Bad at sports and dancing

Centuries of sedentary living and ruling from dark castles have taken their toll.

WHITE PEOPLE

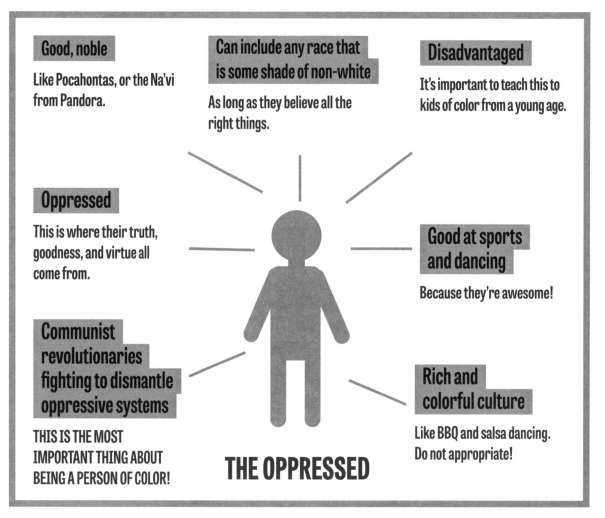

Good, noble

Like Pocahontas, or the Na'vi from Pandora.

Can include any race that is some shade of non-white

As long as they believe all the right things.

Disadvantaged

It's important to teach this to kids of color from a young age.

Oppressed

This is where their truth, goodness, and virtue all come from.

Good at sports and dancing

Because they're awesome!

Communist revolutionaries fighting to dismantle oppressive systems

THIS IS THE MOST IMPORTANT THING ABOUT BEING A PERSON OF COLOR!

Rich and colorful culture

Like BBQ and salsa dancing. Do not appropriate!

THE OPPRESSED

Did you notice we emphasized one of the above features in all capital lettering? That's the most important one. If you have dark skin, are in poverty, and experience oppression but you disagree with the comrades who seek to tear down capitalism, then sorry—you're actually a white person.

Conversely, if you're a white person but you disagree with capitalism, well—you're still a white person, but you are one of the good, useful white people. Racial identity is a one-way street. People of color can become white through assimilation, but white people can never become people of color. They can only become useful.

Here is the best, most simple way to understand race:

Capitalist oppressor=white   Woke, Marxist, communist, dark skin=person of color

See what we did there? We simply associated whiteness with stuff we don't like and non-whiteness with all the stuff we do like! Now, anyone who criticizes your woke ideology is a racist! The great thing about this is a lot of people haven't figured this out yet, and everyone hates to be called a racist. If you can trick people into thinking their very worldview and way of life is racist, you can trick people into giving it up to make way for the woke revolution!

BREAKING DOWN RACISM

The most important rule of racism is that only white people can have it. Under woke definitions, racism requires cultural hegemonic power, which is a fancy way of saying that a secret cabal of crusty white people banded together to create a racist society to protect whiteness. Every minute of every day, they use their cultural power to oppress. Without cultural power, it is impossible to be racist.

To help break it down for you, here's a handy chart that can help you determine what is racist and what is not racist:

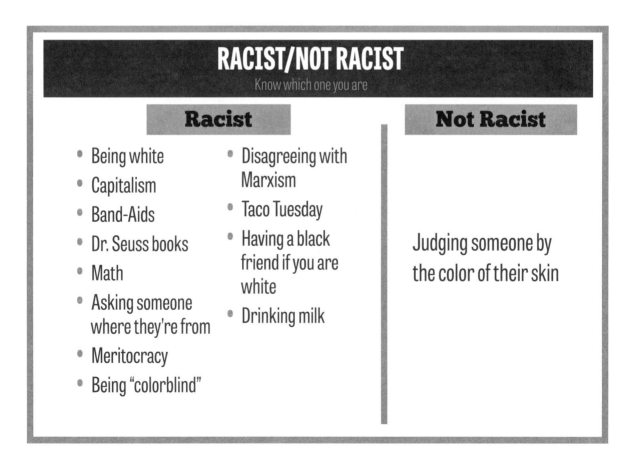

RACIST/NOT RACIST
Know which one you are

Racist

- Being white
- Capitalism
- Band-Aids
- Dr. Seuss books
- Math
- Asking someone where they're from
- Meritocracy
- Being "colorblind"
- Disagreeing with Marxism
- Taco Tuesday
- Having a black friend if you are white
- Drinking milk

Not Racist

Judging someone by the color of their skin

ARE YOU A SECRET RACIST?

You may think you're not a racist. You may think you're one of the good people because you treat everyone equally.

Think again! Racism is bad, but you know what's worse than racism? Secret racism. Many of us who go about our lives thinking we don't hate people for their race are actually secret racists. The racism is just below the surface, simmering like a delicious beef stew in a Crockpot. The kind of stew your mom leaves on for twelve hours and you can smell it simmering throughout the house all day, making your mouth water as you think about dinnertime.

Except the stench wafting through your life isn't beef, carrots, and potatoes: it's right-wing hatred.

It's time to check yourself, educate yourself, and do better. Check how many of these secret signs of racism describe your racist self to a T:

(Please note, this list only applies to white people.)

SECRET RACISM
Know the signs

1. You breathe in oxygen and breathe out carbon dioxide.

Thought you could get away with the racist act of breathing? Think again. Other figures who have been known to enjoy breathing include Donald Trump and Adolf Hitler. What? You read that right: breathing makes you literally the same thing as a Nazi like Trump, or even lesser Nazis like Hitler.

2. You have feet.

Look down—do you see two feet with approximately ten toes? Then you are very similar to all other white supremacists throughout history.

3. You say, "I'm not a racist."

This is an obvious one. If you say, "I'm not a racist" or "I don't hate people for their skin color," you are definitely a racist. Because guess what? That's exactly what a racist would say.

4. You judge people not by the color of their skin, but by the content of their character.

This is a clear sign that you are a far-right racist, as it's a view shared by other racists throughout history. Truly enlightened non-racists know that everything is about race. Well-known white supremacist Martin Luther King Jr. constantly preached this message, so you know it's pretty racist.

5. You like vanilla ice cream.

Vanilla? Seriously? Do you know how far back you're setting race relations in this country? Very bigoted of you.

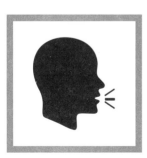

6. You've mispronounced someone's name before—especially a person of color.

Slip up just one time, and you're exposing the festering racism boiling just beneath the surface of your happy-go-lucky exterior. Mispronouncing someone's name is literal violence. In fact, the CDC estimates that more than ten billion people a year die from mispronounced names. Shame on you.

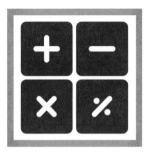

7. You believe 2 + 2 equals 4.

A belief in objectivity, critical thinking, and controversial far-right ideas like two plus two always equals four is a telltale sign of racism. Math has roots in white-colonial-patriarchal ideas, having been a key element in Columbus's figuring out how to sail across the Atlantic. If you believe in objective mathematic facts, you are pretty much a mass murderer.

8. You smile pleasantly and say hello to people of color.

This may look friendly and not-racist on the surface, but what's actually happening here is that you're presuming to enter black and brown genderqueer spaces without first dismantling your own inward supremacy. If you really want BIPOC to feel loved, accepted, and appreciated, distance yourself from them. Don't even acknowledge their existence, really.

9. You don't capitalize, bold, and underline the word BLACK.

This style standard was updated like five minutes ago, but if you haven't gotten on board with it yet, you're still a racist. Also, you must write the word "white" in Comic Sans. (Oh, shoot! We're racists!)

10. You exist.

This is the most telltale sign of racism: you exist. Every racist who ever lived existed, and you're apparently no exception.

Well, looks like you've got work to do, bucko!

DEFINING "WHITENESS"

Whiteness is best understood as "everything bad and evil in the world that we don't like." Some ancient religions have referred to this as "original sin," but that phrase is problematic since it implies that people of all colors, genders, and orientations can be guilty of doing bad things. This is a deeply harmful idea. Oppressed people cannot do bad things. Anything "bad" done by an oppressed person is simply the natural result of their being oppressed. That's why the fault must always lie with the oppressor—and for that reason, the term "whiteness" is a better word to use when describing evil.

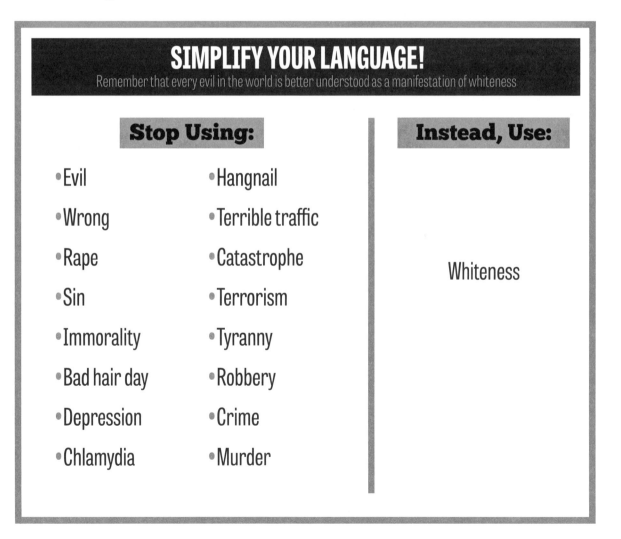

SIMPLIFY YOUR LANGUAGE!
Remember that every evil in the world is better understood as a manifestation of whiteness

Stop Using:

- Evil
- Wrong
- Rape
- Sin
- Immorality
- Bad hair day
- Depression
- Chlamydia
- Hangnail
- Terrible traffic
- Catastrophe
- Terrorism
- Tyranny
- Robbery
- Crime
- Murder

Instead, Use:

Whiteness

Whiteness is the single most dangerous and evil force in the world. Unfortunately, people of color can sometimes become tricked into "whiteness" through a process called assimilation.

GUARDING AGAINST ASSIMILATION

While white people are doomed to remain white for eternity, people of color can actually become white. This can happen in a very problematic process called assimilation. This is when white people capture a person of color and take them to their secret basement to cut open their skulls and replace their natural brain with a brain of white oppression. Once this happens, the victim is effectively white.

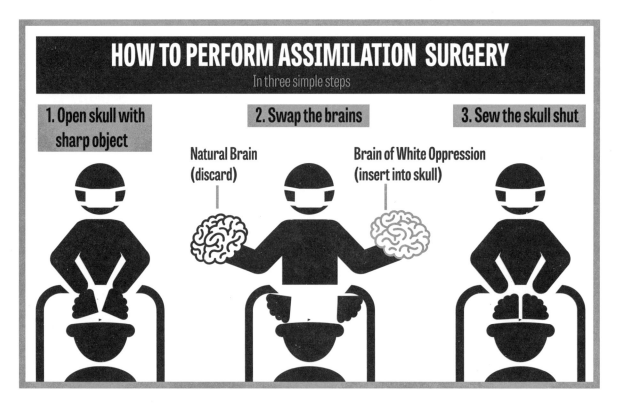

This process is very hard to reverse and must be guarded against at all times.

If a person of color expresses any ideas incompatible with Marxism, queer theory, liberation theology, or abolishing the police, chances are they have been assimilated and are no longer a real person of color.

Some notable victims of assimilation include:

- Ben Carson
- Tim Scott
- Booker T. Washington
- Candace Owens
- Clarence Thomas
- Thomas Sowell

- Shelby Steele
- Larry Elder
- Charles Barkley
- Terry Crews
- Nelson Mandela

To protect people of color from becoming assimilated, we must protect them at all times! They must not be exposed to white ideas or be allowed to enter friendships with unapproved white people. It's our job to be the guardians of blackness at all times and protect our comrades from having their brains removed!

CRITICAL RACE THEORY

Many white people have opposed the teaching of Critical Race Theory at schools and workplaces. This, of course, is because they are dumb. And racist.

Critical Race Theory is a very robust field of study for very smart college-educated people. It is so smart and so robust, in fact, that normal people such as yourself can't understand it. We will do our best to simplify it for you here.

A long time ago, there was the Dark Ages. And then a brilliant man named Karl Marx was born. Before Marx, everyone was like—"Why all the problems? Why bad things happen? Why things not get fixed?" Then, Marx discovered that all of human history can be explained as a struggle between two social classes: the bourgeoisie (rich oppressor) and the proletariat (poor and oppressed).

Karl Marx:
Problem Solver

Marx wrote all this up in a brilliant work called *The Communist Manifesto*, which solved so many problems. In fact—it solved over one hundred million "problems" in the twentieth century alone! Great job, Marx!

Basically, we just took out the long, complicated words "bourgeoisie" and "proletariat" and replaced them with "white people" and "people of color."

Yeah—that's pretty much it. Everything else is mostly unchanged, except we added special bonus "oppression multipliers" people of color can use, such as gender identity and sexual orientation. These multipliers will provide the user with special bonus oppression for even more oppression power!

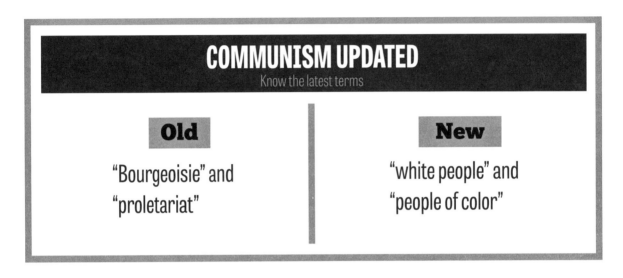

COMMUNISM UPDATED
Know the latest terms

Old

"Bourgeoisie" and "proletariat"

New

"white people" and "people of color"

Under Critical Race Theory:

- **Racism is not an individual attitude, but rather an elaborate, secret system of whiteness used to oppress.**

- **Truth is determined by the skin color and oppression level of the person speaking.**

- **Any "evil" committed by an oppressed person is justified and can actually be blamed on whiteness.**

- **Human beings are reduced to materialist power struggles. How fun!**

The other thing you should know is that Critical Race Theory is the only hope for people of color to live a free and happy life. If we don't entirely reprogram millions of people to think in terms of Critical Race Theory, black people don't stand a chance. They NEED us woke warriors to save them.

BE LESS WHITE

If you really care about the oppressed minorities of the world, you will make every effort to be less white. Coca-Cola and countless other major corporations have instructed their employees to try to de-center whiteness and be less white, and who knows better about being woke than major corporations? Nobody, that's who! So let's work on getting with the program here and being less white!

What does that entail, you may ask? Should you dye your skin darker?

No! Don't do that! We've been through this!

Still, there are ways to ensure that you minimize your whiteness and become less white without resorting to harmful skin-darkening techniques.

HANDY TIPS FOR BEING LESS WHITE
De-whiten yourself today

Burn your "Live, Laugh, Love" signs

In fact, just burn down Hobby Lobby. All of them.

Rip off your skin

Not easy until you start the tear, then it glides right off.

HANDY TIPS FOR BEING LESS WHITE (CONTINUED)

Jump off a cliff

Skyscrapers also work.

Announce that you aren't THAT white

Get some albino friends for maximum effect.

Throw out all your ranch dressing

You and ranch are done.

Take dance classes

Make sure it's not tap dancing or clogging.

Smash your Taylor Swift albums

Then burn the remains.

Buy hot sauce

Garlic parmesan is not hot sauce.

Donate your New Balances to Goodwill

Get rid of any shoes that say, "I'm white."

Just hate yourself forever

Just stare in the mirror and let the hate flow.

MAKE EVERYTHING ABOUT RACE

As we wrap up our discussion on race here, it's important to remember that the discussion on race doesn't ever really end, just like *Goosebumps* sequels, a *Dragon Ball Z* character, or *Fast & Furious* movies. Everything in your life MUST be about race. It must consume everything you do. It must be everything you talk about, everything you think about, everything you breathe, everything you sleep, everything you eat, everything you digest, everything you defecate.

Well, maybe not defecate. But you get the idea: the only way we can truly stop racism is by focusing on race in everything.

This short chapter is just the beginning of your journey to make your entire life revolve around race.

Only then can you stop the racists.

Chapter 3

Feminism and

Gender

Women are oppressed. Before white men came along, women had full human rights and equality. Then white men founded America in 1619 and decided to turn women into chattel for the sole purpose of sandwich-making and bearing children.

Women's liberation is an essential part of the woke movement. While feminists of the past worked to achieve voting rights and freedom from discrimination, they never went far enough because, as it turns out, women are oppressed by definition. There is no way to fully escape oppression if you are a woman. Too bad!

How did the woke movement solve this? We just eliminated women altogether! We do this by:

- Turning women into man-like creatures who sleep around, work grueling corporate jobs, and avoid having kids

- Allowing men to become women, thereby making women irrelevant as a category of humanity

In spite of woke efforts to liberate them, many women still choose a life of patriarchal oppression by becoming wives and mothers. How can you tell whether a woman is oppressed or liberated?

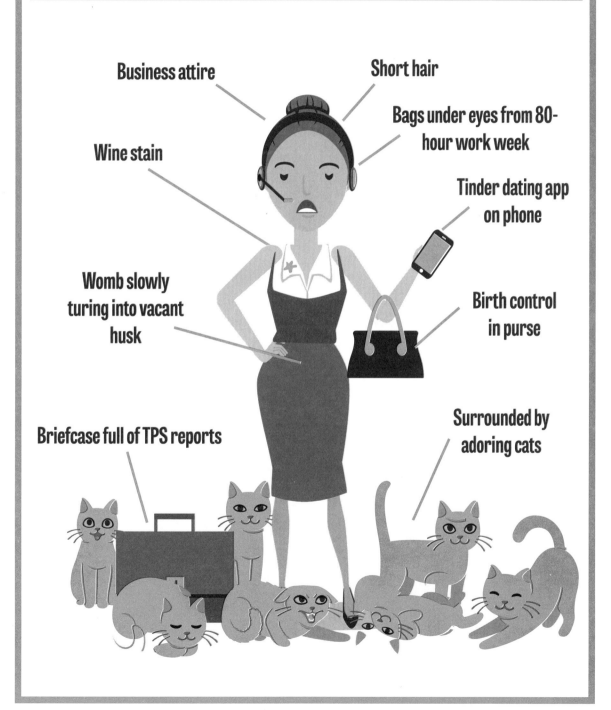

HOW TO BE A FEMINIST

No matter what gender you identify as, you MUST be a feminist if you want to be part of the woke movement.

Identifying as a feminist is very important because it is the only way to show you don't hate women. If you're confused, don't worry! We'll tell you everything you need to know about being a feminist.

Don't get married: It's a trap!

Women need men like a fish needs a bicycle. If you get married to a man, it may trick you into believing men aren't evil oppressors!

Get an abortion

This is one of the most important rites of passage in feminism. Killing your child is the ultimate way to proudly declare your bodily autonomy.

Wear a pink knitted hat to represent your genitalia

For extra feminist street cred, knit your own!

Have lots of cats

These can be stand-ins for the kids you abort.

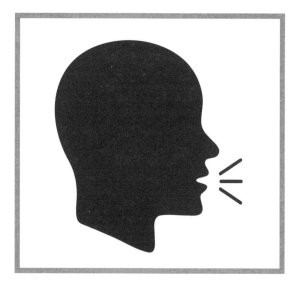

Speak in a very loud, high-pitched voice

This is the only way patriarchal oppressors will be able to hear you.

Shave your head or dye your hair a neon color

Tell the patriarchal universe you don't approve of the hair it gave you! Take it back!

Throw feminine hygiene products at anti-choice politicians

This technique should be used if they don't hear your loud, high-pitched voice.

Scream into the camera for a viral TikTok video

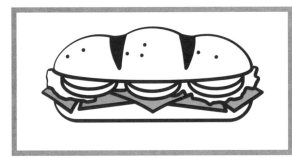

Make a sandwich

Then throw it on the ground to symbolize your liberation.

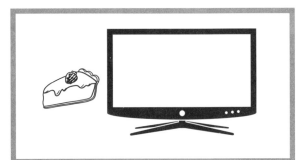

Eat lots of cheesecake while watching Hallmark movies

This will get the patriarchy out of your system after a long day of being a feminist.

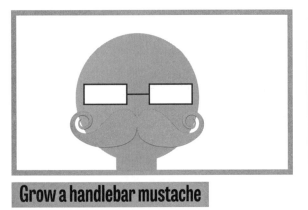

Grow a handlebar mustache

The most masculine of all facial hair.

Take up some casual witchcraft

Take as much birth control as possible

Wash it down with a bottle of wine.

Affirm that trans women are women

Otherwise, you are an evil trans-exclusionary radical feminist—also known as a TERF.

THE LGBTQ+ MOVEMENT

The LGBTQ+ movement is an important part of being woke because—you guessed it—they are very oppressed. For years, they have endured systemic oppression like being thrown in jail or prevented from getting married, but over time it has morphed into even worse oppression—such as people saying things like "I disagree with you" or "My holy book says you're bad." This is NOT OK, people.

We've had some victories over the years, like when Barack Obama lit up the White House in rainbow colors or when Kellogg's released its pride cereal, but there's still so much more we have to do, including:

Ensuring LGBTQ people represent at least 75 percent of all the cast and characters in TV and film

Making sure all sugary cereals are gay

Defeating Mike Pence once and for all

Giving all kids access to essential puberty blockers

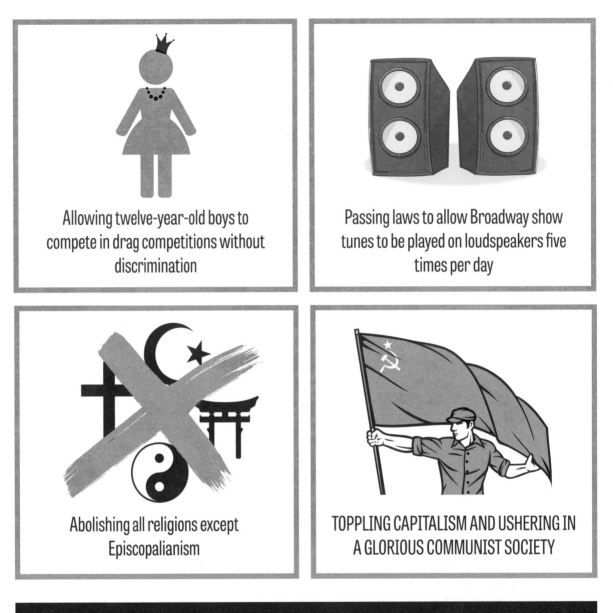

Allowing twelve-year-old boys to compete in drag competitions without discrimination

Passing laws to allow Broadway show tunes to be played on loudspeakers five times per day

Abolishing all religions except Episcopalianism

TOPPLING CAPITALISM AND USHERING IN A GLORIOUS COMMUNIST SOCIETY

LESSER-KNOWN LETTERS IN LGBTQ+

N - NICKELBACK FANS

A - ACCORDIAN PLAYERS

S - SKA ENTHUSIASTS

POS - PEOPLE OF SIZE

P - POTATOGENDERED

H - HARRYPOTTERSEXUAL

O - OMELET LOVER

U - UMBRELLAPHILIAC

$ - BALLER

TRANS RIGHTS

Over time, many people felt that LGB people weren't all that oppressed any more, so we decided to bring in trans people! Boom! We're oppressed again! It's important to note that in order to be properly woke, it's not enough to just accept people who are gay, lesbian, or bisexual. You must also accept the lived truth of trans people. If you don't, that's called being "trans-exclusionary." If you're trans-exclusionary, you may as well be a white male Nazi.

In order to understand trans reality, you must accept the idea that gender is no longer a biological reality, but rather a social construct used to—yes, that's right—OPPRESS PEOPLE.

For thousands of years, people thought gender and sex were the same thing. This is because they were stupid. One day a brilliant intellectual on a college campus discovered that sex and gender were totally different things, and EUREKA! Gender theory was born. Now there are infinite genders you can identify with, no matter what your sex is.

Here is a list of just a few for you to choose from—and don't worry. This isn't an RPG! If you change your mind, you can just pick another one later!

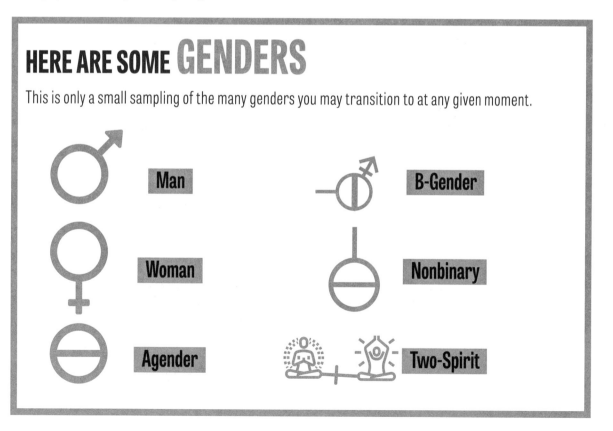

HERE ARE SOME GENDERS

This is only a small sampling of the many genders you may transition to at any given moment.

Man

Woman

Agender

B-Gender

Nonbinary

Two-Spirit

GENERS (CONTINUED)

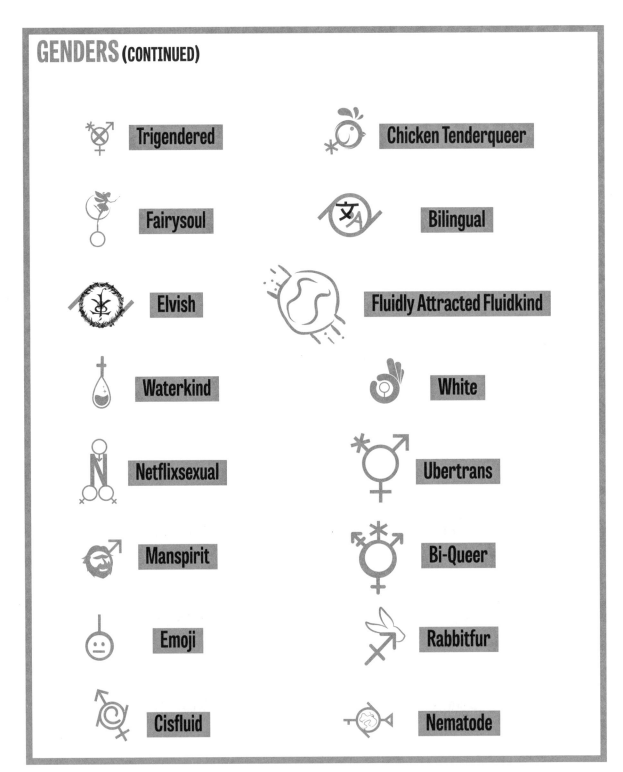

Trigendered

Chicken Tenderqueer

Fairysoul

Bilingual

Elvish

Fluidly Attracted Fluidkind

Waterkind

White

Netflixsexual

Ubertrans

Manspirit

Bi-Queer

Emoji

Rabbitfur

Cisfluid

Nematode

GENDERS (CONTINUED)

Trans-Former

Trans-Fat

Libertarian

Twixsexual

Diet Male

Rhomboid

Male Zero

Combo

Femaleo

Pi

"?"

Male^2

Malex

Pan-cis

Mangirl

Ghostboob

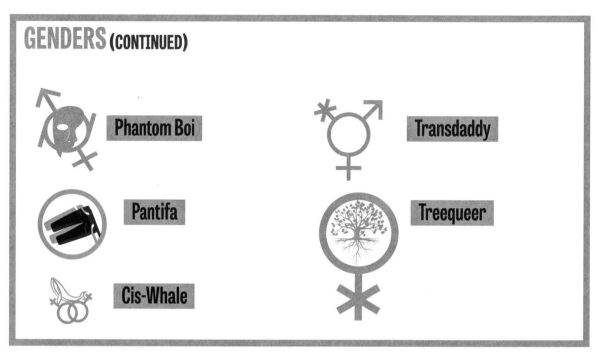

GENDERS (CONTINUED)

Phantom Boi

Pantifa

Cis-Whale

Transdaddy

Treequeer

PRONOUNS

Let's talk about pronouns.

What are pronouns? They used to be simple parts of speech, an easy way to reference something without saying its proper name again and again.

But no longer. Pronouns are now an important part of your noble fight for justice.

Pronouns are everything. They are your badge—the identifying marker that will separate you from the outsiders, the science deniers, and the unbelievers. It doesn't even matter what your pronouns are. If you have them and you display them proudly everywhere you go, that tells everyone you are a good person. **Your pronouns tell others you believe all the correct things about:**

- **Racism**
- **Gender identity**
- **Climate change**
- **Socialism**
- **Religion**
- **Wearing masks to protect from viruses**
- *Star Wars: The Last Jedi*

- **The Israel-Palestine conflict**
- **The answer to 2+2 (hint: it's not 4 anymore)**
- **Mermaidkind polyamory**
- **And many more essential doctrines**

Pronoun usage became popular a few days ago when we decided gender is different than biological sex because, well, duh. Thousands of years of human civilization, science, and culture got it wrong. The world was waiting for us to enlighten everyone.

Let's start with the gender binary. A "female" is someone with two "X" chromosomes. A woman, however, is something completely different. You don't have to be a female to identify as a woman.

How do you know if you're a woman? It's simple! Do you feel like a woman? Then you're a woman! The definition of a woman, of course, is anyone who feels like a woman. "Woman" is just a word that can really mean whatever you want it to mean. You may not be sure whether you feel like a woman since the definition of "woman" comes from whatever feelings that word gives you when you say it.

It's an eternal circle of meaninglessness! Isn't that great? No more meaning! You create it yourself! You are now a god in your own personal reality! Now all that's left to do is pick some pronouns based on how you feel about yourself. Show the world who you are!

If you think this is all a little new and weird, or if you aren't sure you agree with it, that's OK. You should use pronouns anyway in solidarity with the woke. You should also do it so we don't hunt you down and destroy you.

BAD PRONOUNS

While there are billions of pronouns to choose from, there are a few which are not OK and should be avoided. These include:

He/Him	Trump/Trumpself
Beep/Boop/Bop	Dude/Bro
Ptera/Dactyl	She/Her
MA/GA	Y'all/Y'allself
Thee/Thine	He-Man/Him-Man

HOW TO CHOOSE YOUR PRONOUNS

To help you choose the best pronouns for yourself, follow this handy guide:

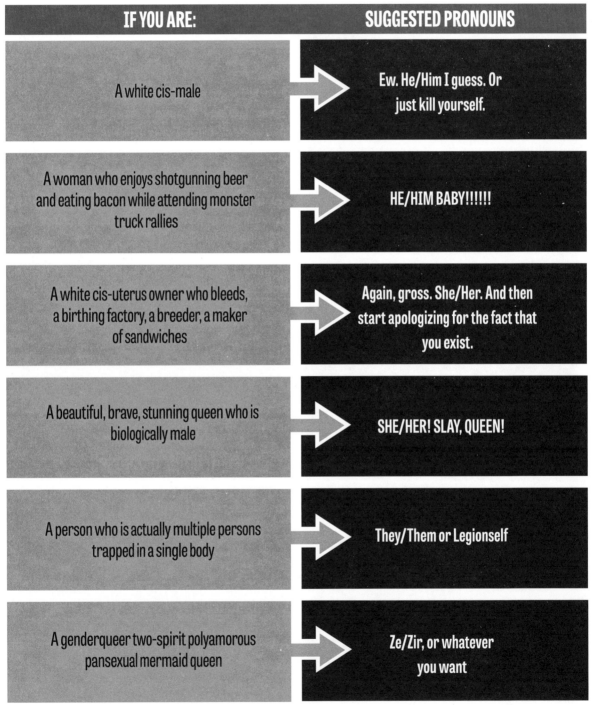

IF YOU ARE:	SUGGESTED PRONOUNS
A white cis-male	Ew. He/Him I guess. Or just kill yourself.
A woman who enjoys shotgunning beer and eating bacon while attending monster truck rallies	HE/HIM BABY!!!!!!
A white cis-uterus owner who bleeds, a birthing factory, a breeder, a maker of sandwiches	Again, gross. She/Her. And then start apologizing for the fact that you exist.
A beautiful, brave, stunning queen who is biologically male	SHE/HER! SLAY, QUEEN!
A person who is actually multiple persons trapped in a single body	They/Them or Legionself
A genderqueer two-spirit polyamorous pansexual mermaid queen	Ze/Zir, or whatever you want

IF YOU ARE:	SUGGESTED PRONOUNS
An amoeba	Gloop/Glop
Sméagol/Gollum	Ourses/Theirses
Donald Trump	REEEEEEEEEEEEEEE!!!!!!!!! (Is he gone? Tell me when he's gone!)
Treebeard the Ent, Groot, or someone who really thinks trees are neat	Tree/Treeself
An undead nightmare who consumes human blood	vam/vamp
Groot	GROOT/GROOTSELF

Again, it really doesn't matter which ones you choose. Words don't have meaning, remember? Just pick some and define them however you want! You can always change them later. The most important thing here is that you pick some and display them prominently. Pronouns are your mark that identify you as being on the right side of history. They are how everyone will know you're woke!

Once you have picked your pronouns, it's important to display them prominently and loudly declare them to every single person or non-person-identifying person you meet.

Once you have your pronouns picked out, it's important to display them so everyone knows you're one of the good people. Here's a guide to displaying your pronouns:

PROCLAIM YOUR PRONOUNS
Here are some ways you can let everyone know how you identify

☑ Prominently display them on all your social media accounts

☑ Always state them to anyone you're introducing yourself to and be sure to repeat yourself twenty or thirty times to make sure they get it

☑ Brand them on your forehead

☑ Engrave them into a signet ring so you can punch them into people's faces like The Phantom

☑ Get a megaphone and scream them into people's ears as they pass by

☑ Hire a stunt pilot to skywrite them above your apartment every day

☑ Carefully spell them out in a hot bowl of alphabet soup—and then throw the soup in a white male's face

☑ Spray-paint them on the driveway of Mike Pence

☑ Go to Costco and loudly announce your pronouns over the intercom

☑ Ask a flash mob to follow you around and do a pronoun dance for everyone who talks to you

Always be on the lookout for people who properly display your pronouns. These are your comrades in your fight against the forces of oppression. Unless, of course, they do something bad or say a mean word that gets them canceled. In that case, not even pronouns can protect them from the righteous fire of our movement—or our Molotov cocktails.

You must also be on the lookout for people who don't display their pronouns, or worse—make fun of those who do. These are bad people and should be considered your mortal enemies. You must hate them and work every day to destroy their lives. It doesn't matter how nice and sweet these people appear. They are outsiders and are not to be trusted. Consciously or not, they are propping up the white Western cis-male system of oppression and must be defeated at all costs.

If someone doesn't use your preferred pronoun, it's OK to tell them you're offended. It's even better if you murder them. Seriously, it's totally justified if you stab someone in the face if they don't say the sacred special word you have chosen.

Remember, this is a war between nice, polite, good people on the right side of history and Nazi-adjacent progress-phobes. It's also a contest between we who define our own reality and people who let their reality be defined by oppressive systems such as nature, God, logic, virtue, and patriarchy. Proclaim your reality and become its vengeful god!

REALITY CAN BE WHATEVER YOU WANT

When it comes to gender, you define the rules. Like Thanos equipped with the Reality Stone, you no longer have to make adjustments to yourself to account for the harsh, brutal reality of life.

You don't have to change the way you live.

You don't have to change the way you think about the world.

You never have to be confronted with the harmful idea that you might be wrong about something.

Instead, make those bigots respect your identity.

Chapter 4
The True Story of
American History

If you're going to be effective as an agent of wokeness, you need to know all about the dark and evil history of America. You may have learned in school that America is all about freedom and equality, but that's a lie perpetuated by ExxonMobil and the Koch brothers.

In reality, America is a deep, dark pit of evil filled with racism and oppression. It was a system designed only for white people, so if you don't have white skin, it's impossible to have a free and prosperous life in America. And if you're a person of color who feels happy and content here, that's only because you've been hypnotized into happiness by white supremacists and the patriarchy.

To fully understand how horribly evil America is, we must go to the very beginning.

(TRIGGER WARNING: This very accurate historical account contains detailed descriptions of oppression and problematicness.)

CHRISTOPHER COLUMBUS

Before there was Hitler, there was someone even worse: Christopher Columbus. In 1492, he disguised himself as a brown-skinned Italian and set sail for America to commit genocide against innocent Native Americans and establish a chain of restaurants called the Olive Garden.

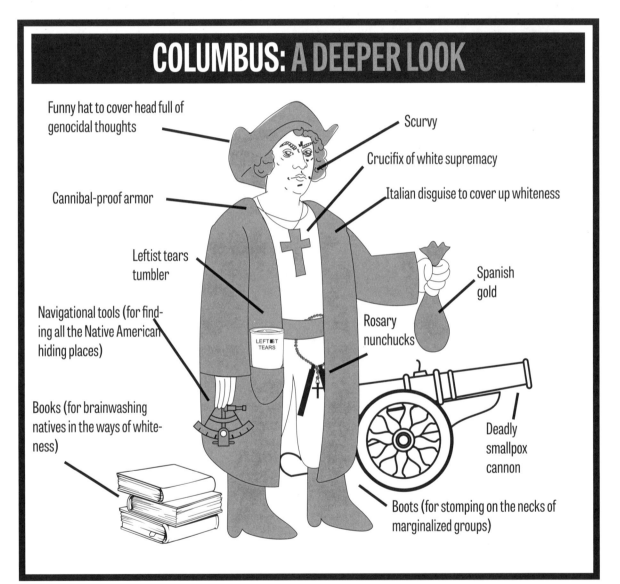

COLUMBUS: A DEEPER LOOK

Funny hat to cover head full of genocidal thoughts

Scurvy

Crucifix of white supremacy

Cannibal-proof armor

Italian disguise to cover up whiteness

Leftist tears tumbler

Spanish gold

Navigational tools (for finding all the Native American hiding places)

Rosary nunchucks

Books (for brainwashing natives in the ways of whiteness)

LEFTIST TEARS

Deadly smallpox cannon

Boots (for stomping on the necks of marginalized groups)

Before Christopher Columbus arrived with smallpox and endless breadsticks, Native Americans lived in peace and harmony with nature and each other. They were beautiful and noble people who would fly around on the backs of mythical winged creatures, come together to dance in a circle around a fire and tell stories, and then finally climb into a giant magic tree and go to sleep, at one with nature.

AMERICA BEFORE COLUMBUS

COMING SOON OLIVE GARDEN

AMERICA AFTER COLUMBUS

They also practiced slavery and genocide on each other, but that was a part of their rich, ancient culture and how dare you judge it. Yeah—we know you were judging. How dare you.

When Columbus arrived, he tore off his Italian brown-skinned disguise and invented white supremacy to oppress all the innocent natives. This is where it all began.

THE PILGRIMS

Over one hundred years after Columbus desecrated the Americas with his whiteness, a large group of Christian fundamentalist homeschoolers set sail to bring homophobia to the land and establish Liberty University.

PILGRIMS: A DEEPER LOOK

Fifteen-passenger van

Thirteen kids because they don't believe in contraception

Tall hat with a buckle on it (to hold in all their bigotry)

White skin, not even disguised this time

MAGA sticker

Make Ye America Greateth Againeth

AYFLR

Homophobic book

Blunderbuss with flared barrel, for maximum genocidal destruction

Chastity belt

Smallpox-infected pumpkin pie

Dorky clothes

When the progressive Native Americans heard that religious extremist Pilgrims were coming, they decided to preemptively kill themselves with the plague so they wouldn't have to deal with all the lame, stuffy Puritans spoiling all their fun.

When the Pilgrims landed, they culturally appropriated one of Mother Earth's boulders and renamed it "Plymouth Rock." They were bummed to find out that all the Native Americans had died and they would have no one to oppress, until they met a surviving Native American named Squanto and tricked him into assimilating into white supremacist culture.

That first winter, half the Pilgrims died of sickness. This was mainly because they were science deniers and refused to wear masks. Sadly, many of these white oppressors survived the winter and established America's first racist holiday: Thanksgiving.

Then they established a Christian fundamentalist indoctrination center called Harvard University. Thankfully, the woke movement has now kicked out all the Puritans, who have since changed locations and established Liberty University.

Thanks a lot, Pilgrims!

1619 AND 1776

White nationalists want you to believe that America was established in 1776, but that's a lie. In 1776, the racist founders of America threw off a tyrannical, slave-trading world power called Great Britain to establish a free and just society for everyone. But they just did that to make you think they weren't racist. Then they secretly went back in time to 1619 to establish a white nationalist society specifically designed to oppress LGBTQ people and people of color.

The Founding Fathers then traveled back to the future in 1787 to write a racist constitution in order to enshrine white supremacy and slavery into our legal system. They took a side trip to the twenty-first century to write the musical *Hamilton*, hoping to deceive future generations into thinking America's Founding was done with good intentions. To their credit, the music was pretty catchy and they hoodwinked many; but after a couple years we saw through that garbage.

The Declaration of Independence says "all men are created equal," but what most people don't know is that there is a secret invisible ink on the document, and when you look at it through special secret racist glasses, it actually says "all men are created equal except black people."

Professional document thief Nicolas Cage exhibits the clearly racist Declaration of Independence that he just stole

Most of the founders were against slavery, and many went on to become abolitionists, but we know they didn't really mean it. Many founders, including George Washington and Thomas Jefferson, actually owned slaves, which means they were hypocrites. Since some of the founders failed to live up fully to American ideals, that automatically means those ideals are racist and rotten to the core.

The founders made a fatal mistake when they filled our Constitution with language and philosophy that would later form the basis of the abolition of slavery and the Civil Rights Movement. They really didn't mean to do that. According to reliable historians, they meant to insert more racist language into the Constitution but forgot to when Ben Franklin's new French girlfriend showed up at Independence Hall to pass out delicious pastries and everyone got distracted. Oops!

MANIFEST DESTINY

After establishing their terrible country, early Americans immediately set about taking over the world. They hired two KKK members named Lewis and Clark to go map out other places to recruit members for the Klan. Lewis and Clark tricked a young Native American girl named Sacagawea into helping them get to the Pacific Ocean, and her stupidity is now forever commemorated on the one-dollar coin that no one uses.

Lewis and Clark, originally spelled ClarKKK

After seeing Lewis and Clark's map, Americans decided the first order of business was to travel into the Great Plains and try to make the buffalo racist. Buffalo, however, are very wise, woke creatures, and since they could not be turned to evil, the settlers instead shot them all.

TRANS BISON ARE BISON

Woke buffalo were nearly wiped out by early settlers

With the plains conquered, America continued its oppression by duping a kindly gay man named Napoleon into selling them the "Louisiana Purchase." Bit by bit, the evil empire expanded.

When gold was discovered in California, capitalist pigs came by the boatload to rob the earth of its shiny treasures. From sea to shining sea, the land of America had become colonized, and as we now know, colonization is one of the great plagues on our land. If only Americans had stayed put in England, all of the badness in the world would be confined to one little, easily canceled island.

TEXAS

Around this time, the most awful, backward place on the surface of the earth came into existence. All of the white supremacists from France, Spain, and Mexico teamed up to make one giant Hydra of oppression, known as the Lone Star State. Spain wised up first, becoming the first nation to cancel Texas. France followed, then finally Mexico—who had to fight a war just to get Texas to leave. In the most famous event of the war, General Antonio López de Santa Anna launched a mostly peaceful protest over Davy Crockett's bigoted refusal to give his pronouns. To this day, Texans like to display their transphobia by periodically screaming "Remember the Alamo!" to recall Davy Crockett's bigotry. Disgusting!

Davy Crockett, Grand Wizard of the Wild Frontier

Antifa taking the Alamo

For a while, Texas became its own country and was defined by such grotesque ideas as "liberty" and "no personal income tax." Cowboys created a toxically masculine culture of independence, and guns—probably AR-15s—were given to children as young as two. America, because it is so awful, naturally wanted Texas to join. Sadly, Texas agreed, bringing all of its climate-destroying oil and cows along with it.

SLAVERY

Even if you're not woke, you know that slavery is bad. Even evil Nazi Republicans agree with us on that one. If we were around in the era of slavery in the South, we would have been the ones to stand up and say that it was wrong. By the way, and apropos of nothing, abortion is totally fine, and if you stand up and say that it is wrong, you hate women.

⊗ **SLAVERY** = BAD   ⊘ **ABORTION** = TOTALLY FINE

Slavery as an insitution was destroyed by a courageous coalition of queer BIPOC freedom fighters disguised as Christians and Quakers. They called themselves "abolitionists." Abolitionists are still around today, except they no longer disguise themselves as Christians and Quakers, and they want to abolish the police. The majority of BIPOC people don't want to abolish the police, but they don't really know what's best for themselves like we do.

Woke BIPOC abolitionists disguised as white Quakers to free the slaves

As far as we can tell, white people are the only ones who have ever practiced slavery. Some white supremacists will try to tell you that Africans and Arabs practiced brutal chattel slavery for thousands of years before America even existed, but we have it on good authority that those slave relationships were entirely consensual, so it was OK.

Racist

THE CIVIL WAR

In the 1860s, a very problematically racist president named Abraham Lincoln decided to free the slaves. Many experts believe this was just his secret plot to have all the slaves to himself. This made all the white supremacists really mad, so they had a war and killed each other for a few years. In the end, about seven hundred thousand white men died to preserve the union and grant freedom to the slaves. Make no mistake though—they were still racists. Dying in the Civil War to free the slaves is sort of like the nineteenth-century version of "I'm not racist because I have a black friend." Nice try, racists.

Anyway, all the slaves were freed, but Abraham Lincoln didn't get a chance to take all the slaves for himself because a guy shot him while he was watching Netflix one night. This is when all the freed slaves were enslaved once again—to capitalism.

THE WORLD WARS

World War I was the result of capitalism, probably. Later, there was the Great Depression. This happened because of capitalism. After the Great Depression came World War II. In this war, we fought against Hitler, who was kind of like a German version of Christopher Columbus. This is also when America fought Japanese people and started the campaign of racist hatred against Asian people. Asian hatred is kind of like homophobia, except not as bad. Many scholars now believe America started these wars to distract everyone from its racism. Absolutely disgusting.

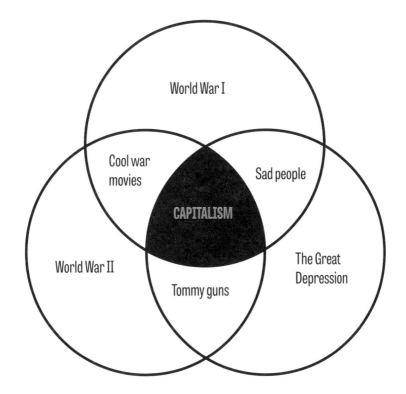

White
Supremacist

THE CIVIL RIGHTS MOVEMENT

The Civil Rights Movement was the worst thing to happen in America since slavery. In it, a right-wing left-wing communist Christian revolutionary liberator and white nationalist named Martin Luther King Jr. encouraged everyone to judge people by their character instead of the color of their skin. Not very woke, MLK! He also advocated for desegregation, which caused whiteness to poison the safe spaces black Americans had worked so hard to build. Tragic.

In the end, the movement won many legislative victories, such as the Civil Rights Act, which was passed by Republicans before the political parties had a secret meeting and decided to trade positions on racism. The worst thing about this movement was that it tricked many people into thinking America had made some progress against racism and discrimination when, in fact, things had only gotten worse—and we have the Civil Rights Act to thank for that. Sad.

OPPRESSION TODAY

Today, America is more evil and racist than ever before. Here are some examples of all the forms oppression takes in modern America:

In some states an identification is required to vote. Clear systemic oppression!

Most Band-Aids are a light skin color

2+2=4: Math is still taught in schools, even though math was once used to count slaves

Texas still exists

Lots of forms still ask you to check a box saying whether you are a man or a woman

We are forced to listen to the national anthem before football games

There's a baker somewhere in Colorado who won't make cakes for gay weddings

We have highways, which our transportation secretary has assured us have racism "mixed into the asphalt"

According to Joe Biden, white supremacists are the #1 most dangerous threat in America, way beyond al-Qaeda, a nuclear North Korea, and mostly peaceful protests

Pride celebrations only last for the entire month of June

Not one single black president since the last black president

In the South, teachers have to work to get paid

People walking down the street are often forced to see American flags

Having to pay for college

A startling lack of black hockey players

Grammar Nazis still oppress people by forcing us to conform to sentence structures

All sorts of standard academic tests

Seats that do not expand to accommodate 700-pound people

Thousands of schools still celebrate "Dr. Seuss Day" to promote literacy

AMERICA IS THE WORST BUT DON'T EVER LEAVE

We've clearly proven that America is the worst place ever in the history of the world. Living literally anywhere else in any other time period would be better.

It's so bad that you'd think we'd move somewhere else with more equitable policies, like Venezuela or North Korea. But instead, we stay here to fight the good fight of making it more like those places.

If you're unlucky enough to live in America with capitalistic oppressions like "high standards of living" and "freedom of speech," we're so sorry. Thoughts and prayers to you. We'd encourage you to constantly threaten to leave for woker places like Canada.

But don't ever actually leave. Just stay here and complain about it loudly and often until policymakers listen to you to score woke points and slowly turn this place into the U.S.S.R.

It's the only way to make up for our racist past.

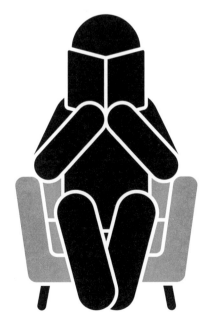

Chapter 5

How to Be Offended by
Everything

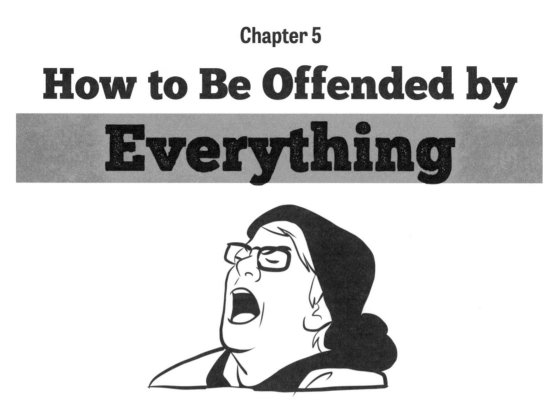

Imagine, **if you will,** the horrors of a world where every little thing doesn't offend you. This isn't a problem for us woke people.

For us, everything can be offensive. Every social encounter, every Netflix show, every trip to the grocery store. Every little thing that happens in life must reinforce the idea that everyone around us is an oppressor and we are innocent, oppressed victims. If this means screaming at the poor minimum-wage employee working at Baskin-Robbins because she didn't use our chosen pronouns, so be it.

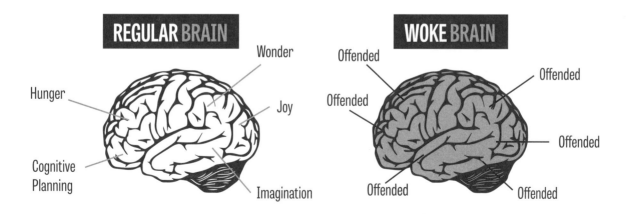

It's part and parcel of being woke. You don't ask if something is offensive—you assume it already is, and then you have to figure out why. It's like a creative writing exercise in your English class—there's no right answer. The real fun is how you get there.

So let's explore some ways to be offended by *absolutely everything*.

MICROAGGRESSIONS

In ages past, oppressed people and minorities had it really bad. They had to deal with slavery, murder, lynchings—all kinds of evil things. (And of course, you carry with you the guilt of every single bad thing every one of your ancestors ever did.)

But remember, no matter how bad they had it, you have it worse. You have to face the horrors of **microaggressions**.

Microaggressions are like attacks on your person, except your attacker doesn't even know they're attacking you. That sounds like it's not as bad as an actual attack, but it's even worse. That person is so racist, sexist, or any of the other -ists that they simply ooze racism out of everything they do, like a grocery bag filled with wet, moldy papayas you left in the trunk of your car for seven weeks and forgot about.

Yeah. Microaggressions are pretty much the worst thing ever to happen to anyone in all of human history. Let's take a look at some of the more common ones:

Breathing

Breathing can be a microaggression. The person is saying, "I am a white oppressor stealing your air and breathing toxic, problematic CO_2 all over you because you are an inferior BIPOC and you should literally die." All of that without ever speaking a word. Wow! Talk about violence!

Existing

Existing is a really bad microaggression, even worse than breathing. Every second you exist, you hatefully occupy space that could be occupied by an oppressed minority. Welp, sorry, man, but there's only one way to take care of this microaggression if you really want to be an ally to people of color! See you in the next life, sucka!

Chewing with your mouth open

Munching cereal with your mouth open and slurping all that milk disgustingly? You are a colonizer of everyone else's ear drums. Stop that!

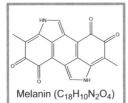

Lacking melanin

If you find yourself having less melanin than others around you, stop. Look. Listen. Be more considerate of your skin color. Be less white (without, you know, doing blackface or anything. That's even worse).

Melanin ($C_{18}H_{10}N_2O_4$)

Telling a minority you appreciate their culture

Picture this horrifying scene: "Hey, Pedro! You're from Mexico, right? I love Mexico! Beautiful country. I especially like the food!" Did you cringe through that whole imaginary conversation? We sure hope so. Because what just happened is that Pedro was microaggressed against, with the (presumably white) speaker othering Pedro by expressing an interest in his culture.

Having a black friend

If you have a black friend, that's a clear microaggression against BIPOC individuals around you. You're basically saying, "Your only value is as a token minority to make me feel better about myself."

Not having a black friend

If you don't have a black friend, that's a clear microaggression against BIPOC individuals around you. You're basically saying, "Black people don't exist, and I don't care about you at all."

Commenting on a minority's ethnicity

To point out that someone looks different than you, has a unique name, or has a cool accent is an obvious microaggression. Do not single someone out like that. Do not appreciate anything interesting or unique about that person. Treat everyone like identical robots. This is the only way to achieve true empathy in our culture.

Ignoring a minority's ethnicity

To just ignore a minority's ethnicity is just as bad as saying you're colorblind. You must comment on their ethnicity. But oh no! That's also a microaggression. Too bad!

RECOGNIZING MICROAGGRESSIONS IN EVERYDAY LIFE

Non-woke people don't even see microaggressions because they are still blinded by their hate.

To them, microaggressions are like eating, drinking, sleeping, or breathing—they just do them naturally.

But woke people see microaggressions in everything.

Let's see if we can spot some microaggressions in these seemingly innocent conversations, and let's learn together how best to respond to these horrible acts of violence against oppressed peoples:

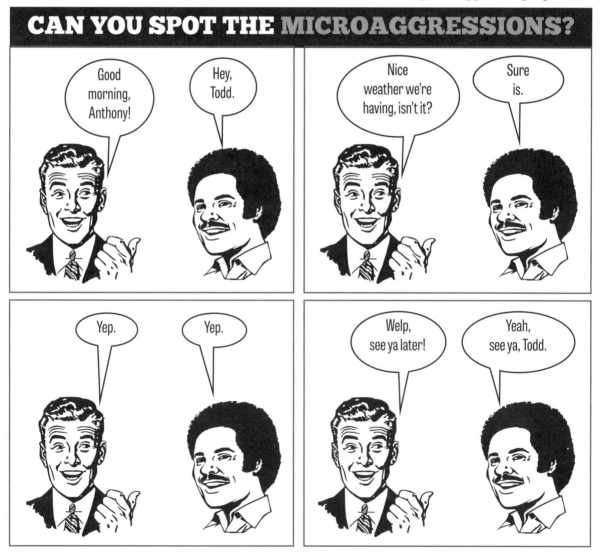

Wow! Let's take a look at all the microaggressions here:

1. **Todd said hi to a person of color,** colonizing his space and asserting dominance as a white supremacist. He might as well have just shot Anthony in the face. This is really offensive.

2. **Todd suggested the weather was "nice," minimizing the struggle of people of color** everywhere. How can the weather be nice when the Republican Party still exists? Of course Todd thinks the weather is nice—he's a racist who's satisfied with perpetuating the status quo.

3. **Todd said "Yep," agreeing with a person of color.** When you smile, nod, and say "yep" to a black person, you're simply patronizing them and suggesting that they need white affirmation before any of their opinions become valid. Very racist.

4. **Todd said, "See ya later!"** callously suggesting that he would be forcing his presence upon Anthony later in the day without even asking for consent. Be silent and let people of color be the ones to initiate the suggestion that you will see them later.

5. **Todd didn't constantly apologize for being white.** Truly woke people will punctuate every sentence with constant apologies for not having the right skin color. Todd didn't do this, further demonstrating that he is complicit in white supremacy. He might as well have worn a KKK hood throughout this conversation—and from all we know here, maybe he was.

6. **Todd never once offered to kill himself to reduce white influence on the world.** This is a common mistake white people make in conversations with BIPOC persons, never being considerate enough to say, "Hey, I'm gonna go ahead and off myself to make the world a better place!" Sad. Not good!

We hope you caught all six of those. There are probably dozens more, but we'll leave you to find them on your own.

RESPONDING TO MICROAGGRESSIONS

Pro Tip: The best way to fight microaggressions is with a good stabbin' knife and high-powered microscope if you can afford it.

All right, so you now know what a microaggression is. We've outlined a few of the more common ones, and we've provided you with a sample conversation containing literally dozens of them.

So how are we supposed to respond to microaggressions when we encounter them in everyday life? First, it's important to remember that microaggressions are literally violence. When someone accidentally pronounces your name wrong, breathes on you, or comments on your culture, they might as well have dropped a piano on your head like Wile E. Coyote. Or they could have just blown you up with ACME dynamite. So it's appropriate to respond in kind.

If someone tries to microaggress against you, take a deep breath, count backward from ten, and then punch them in the face as hard as you can.

Here's an example of how that conversation above should have gone, had Anthony been woke enough to speak out against white oppression.

Isn't that so much better? Finally, there is justice in the world. Great job, Anthony!

8 WAYS TO RESPOND TO MICROAGGRESSIONS

HOW TO FIND SOMETHING OFFENSIVE IN EVERYDAY LIFE

One of the easiest ways to tell woke people from non-woke people is how much systemic oppression you can see in everyday life.

If you're woke, you will see oppression in everything, even if it's not there.

Say it with us: **Everything is offensive if you try hard and believe in yourself.**

Here are some ordinary, everyday objects that appear to be just fine—but to the woke, they're extremely offensive. Hopefully, this exercise will train you to begin looking for systemic racism and oppression in literally everything.

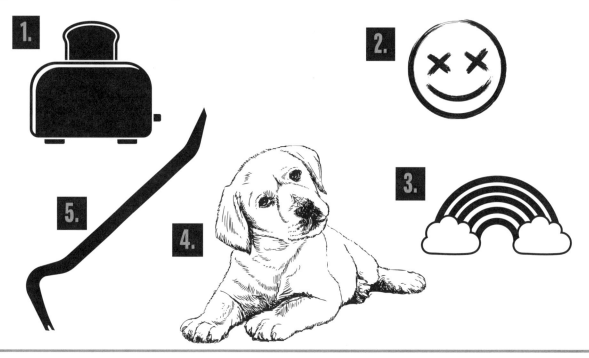

1. **A toaster**—Toasters take slices of WHITE bread and turn them BLACK. Can you say BLACKFACE!?

2. **Smiles**—How can anyone smile when there is evil in the world? Not good!

3. **Rainbows**—God stole the rainbow from the LGBTQ community—a clear case of cultural appropriation.

4. **Puppies**—Sure, they look innocent enough. But they respond to racist dog whistles, proving they are part of the white supremacist movement.

5. **Crowbars**—Racist white man Gordon Freeman used a crowbar to beat illegal aliens from the planet Xen to death.

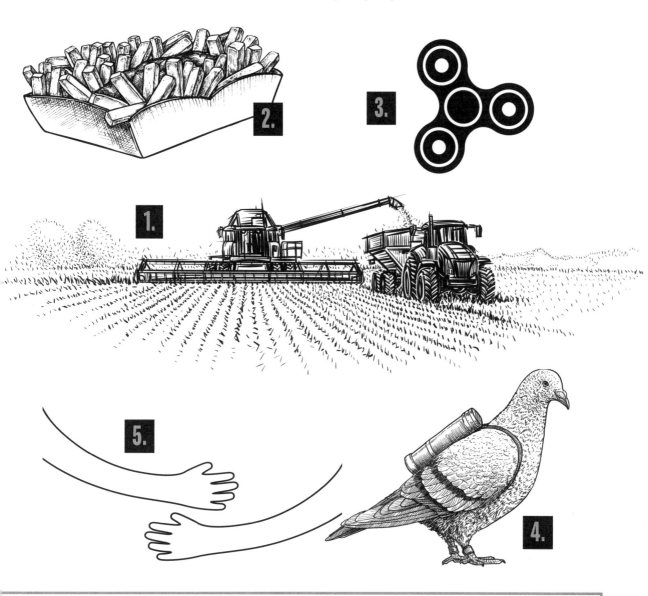

1. **Industrial farming equipment**—These large machines literally rape the earth, triggering millions every time they harvest their crops.

2. **Carne asada fries**—Cultural appropriation and a microaggression against your intestines.

3. **Fidget spinners**—Probably racist.

4. **Pigeons**—Pigeons represent white colonialism because they insist on colonizing everything and pooping everywhere.

5. **Hugs**—Hugs are a holdover from slavery where you would wrap your arms around someone to let them know you owned them.

THE WORLD IS A TERRIBLE PLACE SO GIVE UP NOW.

When you're woke, you realize that the world is a terrible, brutal, awful, offensive place. Now, even the non-woke realize this, but they respond by trying hard to eke out a living anyway.

The truly woke respond by curling up into a fetal position and screaming about everything that doesn't line up with their perception of reality.

Reality should conform to you, not the other way around.

Now go forth and be offended by everything.

Chapter 6

How to Make Sure Your Church Is as Woke as Jesus

Do you go to church? We won't hold that against you, as long as your church is WOKE. Churches, with their dynamic leaders and pliable populations, can be powerful woke allies! Since wokeness requires abandoning the white Western values of logic and reason in favor of fanatical religious fervor, wokeness can be right at home with religious Christians who have decided their God wants them to be WOKE.

Why should Christians be woke? Easy! Jesus was the wokest person who ever lived!

Just think about it.

HOW WE KNOW JESUS WAS WOKE

He was a brown man and a refugee:

Major intersectional points here. We also heard rumors that He may have been a person of size.

He fed five thousand people by raiding a nearby village and forcing them to pay their fair share:

Jesus was the original activist for food justice. And He fed the people bread and fish, completely avoiding climate change–causing red meat!

He refused to slut-shame the woman at the well or the woman caught in adultery:

Our favorite part of this Bible story was the part when He organized the first slut-walk parade for all the temple prostitutes.

He held a political rally and inflamed the masses to seize control of the means of production:

What more proof do you need that Jesus was a tried-and-true socialist? This is definitely our favorite Bible story.

He punched a Nazi:

The Gospel of Marx records this beautiful story of the Lord punching Nazis and then telling them to turn the other cheek for more beating.

He compassionately put the sick and blind on Obamacare plans:

One of the main reasons people believed Jesus was the Messiah was His amazing miracle of putting people on sensible ACA plans.

He hung out with tax collectors to thank them for their work:

It's thought that Jesus hung out with tax collectors to get them to repent of their thievery. But this is wrong. Jesus actually was thanking them for their valuable redistributive services.

Jesus distributed loaves and fish to everyone and then declared Himself General Secretary and sent millions of people to die in the Israeli gulags:

Jesus distributed the food equally, after making everyone wait in a sixteen-hour-long breadline. Then, it was the gulag for the non-believers!

Jesus went into an airplane hangar, overturned all the jets, and then demanded high-speed rail instead:

People think of Jesus as a gentle, kind soul, but He showed righteous anger sometimes, like in this narrative where He flipped over all the fuel-guzzling, carbon-heavy jets and threw His support behind the Green New Deal.

He also forcefully took 90 percent of the rich young ruler's earnings and created free healthcare for all:

A lot of people think this narrative was to show the high cost of following Jesus, but it was actually to show how we should tax the rich by force in order to pay for healthcare and free internet.

In a powerful statement, Jesus triumphantly entered Jerusalem while driving an environmentally friendly Prius:

This was a powerful statement declaring Himself to be the Messiah and also really woke.

When Lazarus died, Jesus raised him from the dead so he could vote Democrat:

Jesus performed this miracle a few times, raising hordes of people from the dead and leading them straight over to the voting booth so they could cast their vote for a Democratic candidate. Democrats are following in His footsteps and are still performing this miracle today.

OTHER WOKE BIBLE CHARACTERS

It wasn't just Jesus who was woke: take a look at these great examples of Bible characters who were woke AF:

Lucifer

He rebelled against the original patriarch and liberated himself. Lucifer is the original woke hero!

Eve

Lucifer's first student, she founded the women's liberation movement. Ain't no one gonna tell her what to do! You go, girl!

Pharaoh of Egypt

He set up hundreds of compassionate women's healthcare facilities in urban Hebrew areas to help them take care of their firstborns.

Onan

He pioneered birth control. We'll leave it at that. Go ask your parents.

Jezebel

She hunted down crazy prophets who were spreading a ton of fake news.

Pharisees

They pioneered the enforcement of strict social-distancing laws. Way to go, guys!

The robbers who beat up the traveler in the story of the good Samaritan

They were just protesting their oppression. We applaud their bravery.

The prodigal son

At least until he chickened out and came back to his overbearing dad.

The Antichrist

A dedicated globalist hero who pioneers tracking technology for everyone's safety.

The harlot riding the beast

Refused to be slut-shamed. Slay, queen!

Ehud

Stabbed his sword right into a fat king, which is basically the patriarchy personified.

Mary Magdalene

Mostly for being a prostitute. She went downhill after that.

WHAT DOES THE BIBLE SAY?

These well-known Bible verses offer pretty good proof too. **Please note: these verses have been updated to reflect correct thinking.**

Blessed are those who don't feel like working,
for they shall be given free money.
Matthew 5:8

Man looks upon the outward appearance, and so does God
because He's not colorblind.
1 Samuel 16:7

What shall it profit a man if he gain the whole world
and nobody seizes his riches?
Matthew 16:26

*In the image of the primordial soup created He him,
black-skinned and white-skinned, created He them.*
Genesis 1:27

*Render unto Caesar what is Caesar's,
namely everything.*
Mark 12:17

*But I say unto you, love yourself, and cancel
those who spew hate speech.*
Matthew 5:44

*In my Father's house, there are many genders. I go to prepare a
racially segregated safe space for you.*
John 14:2

*Learn to do good; seek social justice, correct systemic oppression;
bring social justice to the fatherless, and plead the queer Palestinian's cause.*
Isaiah 1:17

*After this I looked, and behold, a great multitude from every tribe, tongue, nation, skin
color, sexual orientation, and gender identity, standing before the throne of God, for He
had instituted a diversity quota in heaven.*
Revelation 7:9

In spite of the fact that God doesn't exist and the Bible is an ancient document that we should not look to for guidance, it's clear that God and the Bible both tell you to be woke—so you should obey and be woke. It's as simple as that!

HOW TO GUIDE YOUR CHURCH ON ITS WOKE JOURNEY

What follows is a guide to leading your church into deeper levels of wokeness. **(IMPORTANT: If your church is new at this, only start with racial and political wokeness. Leave gender theory to the side for now. Once your church is thoroughly woke in the area of race and politics, it will be easier to transition to sexual wokeness. Patience, comrade!)**

Go through the entire Bible and find every use of the word "justice." Then simply insert the woke buzzwords such as "social" in there.

"Learn to do good; seek **[social]** justice, correct **[systemic]** oppression; bring **[social]** justice to the fatherless, and plead the **[queer Palestinian]** widow's cause." (Isaiah 1:17)

"But let **[social]** justice roll on like a river, and **[race-conscious]** righteousness like a never-failing stream **[of wealth redistribution]**!" (Amos 5:24)

Social justice pretty much means the opposite of boring old regular justice, but most of the people in church don't know that. Just throw out these verses and they'll follow right along!

Fire all the white male pastors and replace them with women and people of color.

If you attend the average white American church, you have been given an incomplete Gospel. A complete Gospel can only be attained by hearing from a diverse set of voices and lived experiences! Jesus never meant for you to sit under the preaching of some white guy as he preaches from the Bible; He meant for you to gather in diverse spaces and imagine a better tomorrow as a community of radical socialists! Theology doesn't matter when choosing your new church leadership. The most important thing is that you hear from marginalized voices who will enrich your understanding of other truths.

Keep in mind, if you try to correct the theology of a woman or person of color, that is an ungodly imposition of power. Jesus would never do something like that. Your white Christianity is only one way to understand the Gospel.

After you hire your new staff, learn to keep quiet and LISTEN. Make sure you hire marginalized people with a good understanding of liberation theology/communism. If you hire marginalized people who don't like liberation theology, they are fake marginalized people who have assimilated into whiteness. Such people should not be trusted.

Remember, the end goal here is to be like Jesus by turning your regular church into a communist indoctrination center. That's what the Gospel is all about!

Ask God to return all the guilt and shame He took away when all your white members became Christians.

Are you white? Did God take away your guilt and shame? Yup, that was a mistake. He needs to give that back. Guilt and shame are important tools to ensure your congregation remains silent as you make these changes in the church.

Make sure to preach long sermons on the collective guilt of whiteness until your church members feel totally rotten about all the bad things other white people did in the past. The great thing about collective guilt is it can't be forgiven without collective action! Unlike individual sins that people can confess to God, collective sins can only be atoned for by gathering together as a collective political movement to correct perceived power imbalances! Placing a heavy burden on your white members will ensure they keep eating out of your hand in hopes of relieving that guilt. As Jesus said:

"Come to me, all you who are weary and burdened, and I will give you additional burdens! Take my yoke upon you and learn by reading *White Fragility*, and listening to the lived experiences of marginalized people, for I am a revolutionary liberator, and you will find white guilt for your souls. For my yoke is a burden and it's not light." (Matthew 11:28–30)

Segregate your worship center.

Yes, the Bible says every "tribe, tongue, and nation" will worship around the throne, but it never says they will do it together in the same space. Seriously, that would be insane! Whiteness is an inherently hostile presence that always wants to invade spaces meant for marginalized people. Since God is woke, we know He would never erase oppressed people by forcing them to mix and assimilate with white oppressors in His Kingdom. Segregation is SACRED to God. Race is SACRED in God's Kingdom. Your church should look just like the Kingdom.

Make the transition from the Bible to peer-reviewed sociology books.

Now that you've used the Bible to make your church more woke, your church is ready to start listening to REAL wisdom from peer-reviewed sociologists. The academic peer-review system is widely known as the most reliable source of divine truth and is infallible in all its teachings. If someone who is not peer-reviewed attempts to teach you, let him be anathema, for he is a wolf in sheep's clothing—and probably a white supremacist.

Finally, never stop progressing.

The revolutionary's work is never done. If you're careful and patient, you will transform your church from a bastion of white supremacy to a powerful political liberation movement! It worked with the Catholic Church in Venezuela, and today Venezuela is an oasis of socialist equity and fairness. Transform your church and be on the right side of history. You can do it!!!

ADVERTISING YOUR WOKENESS

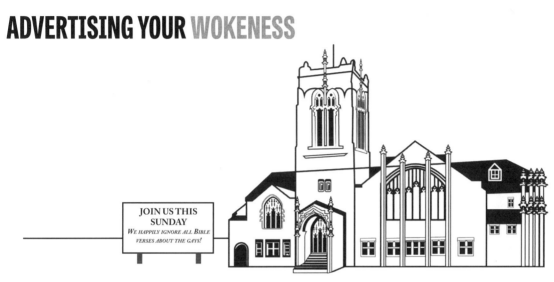

Now that your church is WOKE, it's time to let everyone know! We know you religious types love to virtue signal, right? Here are ten ways to proclaim your church's wokeness:

Set up a wacky, wild, and inflatable arm-flailing tube man outside that says "Black Lives Matter" on it

Preach your entire sermon while taking a knee

ADVERTISING YOUR WOKENESS (CONTINUED)

Replace the cross on your steeple with a giant raised fist

Have the worship team lead the congregation in singing "Imagine" by John Lennon

Have an indigenous worship Sunday complete with war paint and totem poles

Drag Queen Sunday School Hour! (advanced stages of wokeness only)

Have the entire church kneel before a giant black square

Replace all the pictures of white Jesus with pictures of black Jesus

Go into town to smash windows for justice while inviting people to church

Replace all Bibles with the latest Robin DiAngelo book

Your church is a powerful means of wokeness.

It should be obvious by now that it's totally cool to be a Christian—as long as you put wokeness first.

There was a wise (and woke) old philosopher named Screwtape, and here's what he had to say about this:

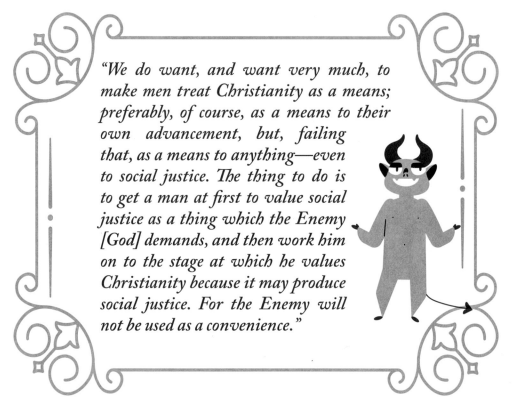

"We do want, and want very much, to make men treat Christianity as a means; preferably, of course, as a means to their own advancement, but, failing that, as a means to anything—even to social justice. The thing to do is to get a man at first to value social justice as a thing which the Enemy [God] demands, and then work him on to the stage at which he values Christianity because it may produce social justice. For the Enemy will not be used as a convenience."

Wow—this guy was pretty smart! That's exactly what Christianity is good for: making people care about our pet causes.

Now it's time to go to church! Or not. Whatever. We really don't care.

Chapter 7

Follow the
SCIENCE

> "The good thing about science is that it's true, whether or not you believe in it."
> —*Neil deGrasse Tyson*

Hundreds of years ago, people followed religion. Today, we follow SCIENCE, which is smarter and far superior to religion and must replace religion in every corner of society.

SCIENCE is a mysterious and divine force in the sky that gives us truth, wisdom, and understanding of the world around us. A good disciple of wokeness will always follow the SCIENCE. They will also—like we did here—always capitalize the word SCIENCE out of respect and fear. We wouldn't want SCIENCE to strike us down in its anger!

The divine words of SCIENCE are brought down to us by infallible people in white coats called "scientists." Scientists are always in complete agreement with each other, forming a vast consensus. If anyone makes a truth claim endorsed by a "consensus of scientists," you must always accept that claim without question. If you don't, you are a SCIENCE denier. You do not want to be on the wrong side of SCIENCE. That's almost as bad as being on the wrong side of history!

So—what are the scientists telling us right now?

They're telling us that if we don't change our ways, we are headed for destruction: climate destruction.

CLIMATE JUSTICE

"Human beings are a disease, a cancer of this planet. You're a plague, and we are the cure."
—**Agent Smith**, *environmental justice activist, sentient computer program*

You may be wondering what the climate has to do with being woke. The one-word answer to this is EVERYTHING. Every sin against wokeness causes climate change, and every injustice in the entire world can be traced back to both climate change and whiteness. Whiteness and climate change are like a symbiotic cycle of pure evil.

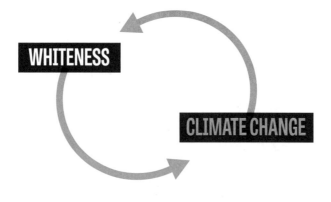

You need to be white to be racist, but climate change is slightly different than racism, even though both are manifestations of whiteness. The only thing necessary for you to be guilty of climate offense is to be a living human being. If you have human DNA and breathe air, YOU are part of the problem.

This element of collective human guilt is what gives our woke movement an extra shot of religious fervor. Religious fervor is essential to maintaining momentum for this movement.

Every religion has three major hooks to draw in new converts.

In wokeness, racism provides guilt, and the LGBTQ movement provides acceptance. Climate change provides us with a wonderfully terrifying doomsday prophecy.

These three things are the three legs upon which the stool of justice rests.

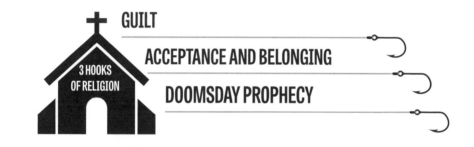

3 HOOKS OF RELIGION

- GUILT
- ACCEPTANCE AND BELONGING
- DOOMSDAY PROPHECY

THE STOOL OF JUSTICE

JUSTICE

RACIST GUILT · LGBTQ SOLIDARITY · CLIMATE CHANGE ACTIVISM

You can't be a true anti-racist ally without also being a climate activist. You can't be a true climate activist unless you also stand in solidarity with the LGBTQ movement. As with any religion, you can't pick and choose what you care about here. You must care about it ALL. If you don't, you're an imposter—and we will find you and cancel you.

The stool of justice can also be used to beat Nazis.

WHAT IS CLIMATE CHANGE?

Climate change is the result of centuries of white cis-male heteronormative Christian patriarchy exploiting the planet for precious recources. Not only that, but they emit CO_2 into the atmosphere. Mother Nature hates CO_2 and gets mad when we spew it out. We literally breathe out this stuff. When you think about it, every time you exhale CO_2 from your lungs, you are literally raping the earth.

Yeah, that's right—you raped the earth, like, twelve times while reading that last paragraph. Your very existence is problematic.

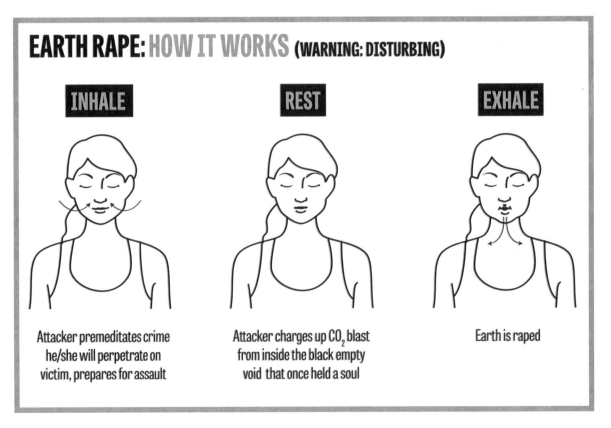

EARTH RAPE: HOW IT WORKS (WARNING: DISTURBING)

INHALE   **REST**   **EXHALE**

Attacker premeditates crime he/she will perpetrate on victim, prepares for assault

Attacker charges up CO_2 blast from inside the black empty void that once held a soul

Earth is raped

According to 103 percent of scientists, Mother Nature will soon get so mad at people for raping the earth that she'll make our sea levels rise, which will cause horrible famines followed by zombies and killer *kaiju* lizards from the sea. Only those who are faithful to wokeness will have the power to prevent this horrific end to humanity. That said, humanity's ending horrifically wouldn't be such a bad thing, since humanity's existing is the greatest threat to the climate. But wouldn't you rather end humanity on your own terms, with you and your woke friends at the top of the totem pole?

WHAT CAUSES CLIMATE CHANGE

Capitalism:

Capitalism may look like an innocent system of liberty in which people freely exchange goods and services, but in reality, it's an oppressive system of oppression created by white people. Not only does it create inequality, but it also allows humans to thrive off the greedy pillaging of the earth. Every time you sell something on Craigslist or buy an Icee at the gas station, the earth sheds a tear. How does that make you feel?

Whiteness:

Fundamental to the philosophy of Whiteness is the slave/master mentality: that the earth is here to serve us. The earth is not your slave! Whiteness must be dismantled so the world will know that we are the earth's slaves, not the other way around!

Cow Farts:

The United States used to be filled with beautiful buffalo, which were completely carbon-neutral. The white man brought with him the cowboy, and with the cowboy came cows. Every single cow is a greenhouse gas-producing monster that wants to turn the atmosphere into a sweltering dutch oven.

Your Existing:

Speaking of carbon footprints, you have one. A massive one. Your very life is an affront to Mother Earth. Have you tried not existing? Maybe try that.

WHAT CAUSES CLIMATE CHANGE (CONTINUED)

Racism:

This is one of the chief drivers of climate change. Racism isn't judging people by the color of their skin. According to the latest definition, racism is just another name for capitalism. If we can get rid of capitalism, racism will go away. If racism goes away, climate change disappears. It's that simple.

Homophobia:

Being straight and cisgendered is homophobic and transphobic. Straight cisgendered people tend to produce CO_2-spewing children. Not good! Homophobic people support things like electroshock gay conversion therapy, which typically runs on coal power. Double not good.

Low Taxes:

Taxes are one of the greatest tools of collective action against climate injustice. When taxes fall, justice falls. Remember that. Better yet, write it on a sign and go scream in the street in front of ExxonMobil's headquarters.

Freedom:

The Christian Bible says "Where freedom abounds, whiteness abounds all the more" (paraphrased). Freedom is a tool used by white supremacists to fill the earth with capitalism and cheeseburgers. The Soviet Union was very good at limiting freedom, and as a result, limited the impact of humans on the climate. Except for the whole Chernobyl thing.

Hamburgers:

The founder of Wendy's, Dave Thomas, may seem like a sweet old man who liked to make a good burger, but did you know he was actually a sinister menace who promoted the mass production of greenhouse gas-producing cows? Dave Thomas was worse for the environment than Hitler was. Come to think of it, Hitler was great for the environment since he reduced humanity's carbon footprint by millions of people. Makes you think.

The Nuclear Family:

Similar to the threat of homophobia, the traditional family tends to produce human kids. You think cows are bad for the climate? Kids are ten million times worse. Especially if they're white.

THINGS YOU CAN DO TO COMBAT CLIMATE CHANGE

Kill yourself:

This is one of the most effective ways to minimize your impact on the planet. You will produce hundreds of thousands of units of CO_2 over your lifetime. Imagine what a difference you could make if you just casually jumped off a bridge or something! We would totally do it, but we need to stay alive to show you and others how to be woke.

THINGS YOU CAN DO TO COMBAT CLIMATE CHANGE (CONTINUED)

Kill someone else:

If you really want to go the extra mile, kill other people to really make a difference! People like Genghis Khan burned and pillaged through Asia, killing much of the world's population so the trees could grow again. He may have delayed climate catastrophe for centuries! Not all of us can be like Genghis Khan, but we can each do our small part! When Cain killed Abel, he wiped out hundreds of generations and greatly reduced the population of the earth at the time! Do your part today!

Get an abortion:

Even better than killing a full-grown carbon producer is killing one before it even gets the chance to produce carbon!

Eat bugs:

If you enjoy bacon or double cheeseburgers, repent, for you are in sin. Eat bugs instead. Did you know that termites alone produce dangerous levels of greenhouse gases on par with human activity? We can't eat bugs because we're allergic, but you definitely should.

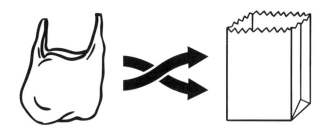

Switch from plastic bags to paper bags:

Plastic bags are horrible for the environment. Switch to paper until all the lumber in the Amazon rain forest is depleted and then switch over to reusable paper bags made by slave labor in China.

Drive an electric car:

Abandon fossil fuels and drive a much cleaner electric car! Once you realize electric cars run on power from coal plants and that lithium batteries use child labor to pillage the earth for lithium, switch to getting around on a horse. Once you realize horses create methane gas and use land resources, get rid of the horse and switch to walking. Once you realize walking increases your breathing rate as well as the CO_2 you exhale, then it's time to see our first tip in this list.

Pay more taxes:

Taxes solve everything. Every time you pay taxes, the money goes into a special climate machine where it is turned into fairy sparkle dust that is shot into the atmosphere to kill all the CO_2. They also help pay Al Gore's salary. Important.

Embrace communism:

Communism basically just means everyone sharing and being really nice to each other. It's the opposite of capitalism, which means it must be good. Communism takes care of almost all the causes of climate change: capitalism, cow farts, the nuclear family, and your existence. In the twentieth century alone, communism removed one hundred million carbon footprints from the earth—well, technically two hundred million carbon footprints, assuming each person had two feet. Thanks, communism!

You're on your way, champ! Take some steps to save the planet today!

CHRISTIANITY: SCIENCE'S GREATEST ENEMY

If you want to stay true to the cause of climate justice, you must understand that Christianity is dangerous to the effective study of SCIENCE.

Everyone knows that if it weren't for Christianity, the scientists would have solved all our problems and we'd have flying cars by now.

Here are seven important ways Christianity completely ruined SCIENCE for everybody:

A Christian discovered gravity, which keeps everyone helplessly pinned to the earth:

Gravity holds everyone down and prevents us from flying in the sky like a flock of pretty birds. Thanks a lot, Newton.

Christian scientists worship God, which makes other scientists feel a little guilty when they want to play God:

Thanks, but we'll pass on the guilt trip, thank you very much.

Christians created antibiotics, which have ruined the process of natural selection by saving lives:

Really—do we need all those old people? SCIENCE says probably not. Survival of the fittest, grandma!

God created the world from nothing, really making everything scientists have accomplished since then look pretty silly:

God is literally saying that SCIENCE isn't that important, since He won't even let scientists create matter out of nothing. He gave the universe a definite beginning, so they can't even really deny it was all created at some point. Sad!

Christianity contributes to the harmful overpopulation of Mother Earth by yucky humans:

We know people are the biggest threat to the earth, but Christians keep wanting to protect them, even the unborn ones. They also have a lot of babies and perpetuate the human race. Ignorant!

The scientific method was created by a devout Christian, which burdens scientists with restrictive fundamentalist rules:

The scientific method limits SCIENCE. We're tired of fundamentalist Christians always imposing strict rules. Live a little, for goodness' sake!

Christianity gives people a transcendent meaning and purpose outside themselves, which is totally lame and anti-SCIENCE:

SCIENCE would be so much cooler if we could explore ideas like eugenics, DNA tampering, and creating a race of robots to enslave humanity without worrying about morals and objective truth. What could go wrong?

GOOD SCIENCE VS. BAD SCIENCE

Over the centuries there have been heretical "science" movements that have sprung up, claiming to be real SCIENCE. This has led to many problematic discoveries that have held back the march of wokeness.

As a follower of wokeness, you must train yourself to have the discernment to tell good SCIENCE from bad "science." Simply put, if it doesn't advance the woke agenda, the "science" is false and should be rejected.

Bad Science   Good SCIENCE

Biology: The heretical study of biology has led many false scientists to claim there are only two genders. These false teachers must be rebuked!

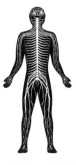

The study of transracial neurodivergent kink ableism and its impact on performative cis-queerness in a BDSM context: Now THIS is SCIENCE. Those who study this noble, peer-reviewed discipline will increase in wokeness.

Diet and nutrition: This false field of study has led to rampant fat-phobia and an unfounded bias toward exercise and healthy eating.

Challenging feminist-exclusionary fat stigma in BIPOC musical theatre: Feminist-exclusionary fat stigma is a growing threat, and it can only be combatted with SCIENCE.

Bad Science   Good SCIENCE

Meteorology: These "scientists" have the hubris to think they can predict the weather days in advance. Plus, meteorology is used to help planes fly safely, which pollutes the atmosphere.

Everything Greta Thunberg says: This divine child of light has been gifted with secret knowledge of what the weather will be like one hundred years from now. Heed her words, or deny them at your peril.

Physics: This problematic field of study of the unchangeable laws of the physical universe leads to the rigid either/or thinking that is a prominent feature of whiteness.

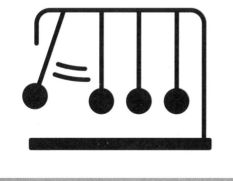

The history of pop-culture biphobia and underage Anglo-Muslim sexuality in the TV show *Friends*: Ivy League classes across the country are offering this course, and it's about time!

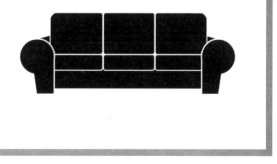

Are you starting to get it yet?

The most important litmus test for SCIENCE is whether or not it helps you dismantle Western civilization and prevent climate Armageddon.

Now go forth, believe, and follow SCIENCE. May its name be praised.

Chapter 8

How to Fight Fascism
with Violence

Nazi
(probably)

OK, so you're on board with us now when it comes to this whole woke thing. You're believing the right things, you've shaved off half your hair and dyed the rest purple, and you've even selected some really special pronouns. You're simply wallowing in guilt for your complicity in normalizing and perpetuating toxic white privilege and systemic oppression against LGBTQIA+ BIPOC through your ignorant participation in capitalist society.

Wow. You're doing great!

BUT, AS ALWAYS, YOU NEED TO **DO BETTER**.

DO BETTER: USE VIOLENCE

As we've already pointed out, wokeness isn't a private religion you can keep to yourself. Once you see the world through woke eyes, you'll never be the same, and you'll never be able to stop telling your friends about your new beliefs.

So we need to spread the good news to people out there. We need to take to the streets in order to stop the Nazis.

And how are we going to do this exactly?

Well, the only surefire way to fight fascism is by using violence against our enemies.

We're anti-fascist experts, so we have tons of helpful hints and strategies to defeat the Nazis once and for all by punching people we don't like in the face.

ARM YOURSELF WITH SOME VIOLENT WEAPONS

The first step to fighting fascism is equipping yourself with the right tools. Just as a soldier wouldn't go into battle without his trusty sword, so brave anti-Nazis can't destroy fascism without the most violent weapons available.

Here are a few weapons to always have on your person at all times:

Bricks

If you're going to fight fascism, you should start by picking up some bricks. They're low-cost and very effective at creating violence and destruction of property—two essential elements for the person fighting Nazis.

Bike Locks

Great for beating fascists. You can get a lot of momentum on the end of one of these bad boys as you swing it around like Mikey from the *Teenage Mutant Ninja Turtles*.

Soup Cans

Bring a soup can everywhere you go so you can throw it at some police officers. Then, when you get caught with it on your person, you can say you were just carrying some soup to take home to your family. Just make sure it's vegan, fair-trade, locally sourced soup. Or you're no better than the Nazis.

Fists

Can't afford a brick? Just use your fists—they accomplish the same thing, but they're more intimate and personal.

Cement Milkshakes

Cement milkshakes are delicious and destructive. Just make sure they're soy-based and vegan.

Molotov Cocktails with "Coexist" Stickers on Them

What better way to show how inclusive and pro-social justice you are than by burning down some neighborhoods with your "Coexist" Molotov cocktails? Every building you burn to the ground is further evidence that you're on the right side of history.

FORCE PEOPLE TO BELIEVE THE SAME THING AS YOU

One of the best ways to weed out bad ideas is to make sure everyone believes the same things as you. Unfortunately, people are stubborn, and they don't like to just automatically agree with you on everything. So, we have to use force—you know, to stop the Nazis.

Ideological conformity is an essential part of any anti-fascist activist's tool kit. One of the best ways you can make sure fascism doesn't rear its ugly head again is to enforce complete ideological agreement across the board. If people aren't complying, go back and reference our list of violent weapons—these are all great tools to force your ideas on other people.

CONFORMITY MADE SIMPLE

| Problem: | Solution: | Outcome: |
| This person will not conform to your beliefs | Throw a brick at their head | They now will conform to your beliefs |

THE INTERNET

One great way to force your ideas on others is to cancel them using the power of the internet. Those fighting Nazis in decades past only had simple tools like howitzers and hand grenades But now we have the World Wide Web and social media. If you're trying to stop the white supremacists, pull up Twitter, find bad tweets from people you don't like, and get them canceled. They'll lose their job and be run out of polite society, and you'll feel smug and virtuous. It's a win-win.

Historians say that if Hitler had had the internet, he would have been much more dangerous and probably would have been called Adolf Twittler.

TAKE TO THE STREETS

Sometimes, your righteous hate for Nazis might even drive you outside your parents' basement. You might need to take to the streets to fight the bad guys, just like those brave men on D-Day in 1944.

Yep—you can be literally as brave as a D-Day soldier if you're only willing to take to the streets to fight the Nazis. Protesting for social justice—especially mostly peaceful protesting—is pretty much the same thing as storming the beaches of Normandy to oust Hitler from Europe.

But how do you effectively protest against the Nazis? In decades past, protesters used to calmly walk down the street and hold signs, chanting catchy slogans.

But now, we have more ways to take to the streets to fight the Nazis.

MORE WAYS TO FIGHT THE NAZIS

Force people to do your special salute

If you really want to make sure your city or town is free of fascism, come up with a special salute. You could, say, raise a fist up in the air. Or, if holding it that high is too hard, just hold it up at a 45-degree angle. Then, go through the streets and make sure everyone else is doing your salute. If not, you know what to do: IT'S BRICK TIME!

March down the street in lockstep

Want the Nazis to be shaking in their boots? Try marching down the street in perfect lockstep. When people see how fearsome you and your ranks of fellow anti-fascists are, they'll give up their Nazi ways.

Chant slogans in unison

Select your favorite woke slogan: BLACK LIVES MATTER! Or perhaps something reasonable and peaceful like ALL COPS MUST DIE! Then, make everyone else chant the slogan along with you. This will definitely end fascism.

Burn books

The problem with books is that they contain ideas. Sometimes, they contain bad ideas. While in ages past, people would argue with bad ideas and prove just how bad and dumb they were, this has its drawbacks. Because then if you believe dumb things, your ideas might get exposed too. And then you'd have to start rethinking things and maybe adjusting your worldview. But there's a solution to this that helps us fight the Nazis without having to debate: a good, old-fashioned book burning. Find books you disagree with—be they biology books, math textbooks, history books, or Dr. Seuss books for children—and burn them. That way, Nazism can never spread again.

Burn down minority-owned businesses

Any good Antifa member knows that you have to burn down neighborhoods in the name of justice. But it sucks to burn down your own neighborhood, because then you can't chill and play Xbox. Since, you know, your parents' house has been burned to the ground. So, the best way to burn down neighborhoods for racial justice is to go to a minority neighborhood nowhere near where you live and incite a riot. George Soros might even pay for you to make the trip—score!

ANTIFA WEAKNESSES   Know your own kryptonite

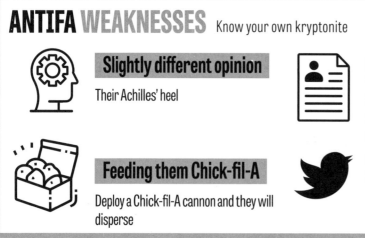

Slightly different opinion
Their Achilles' heel

Job applications
Antifa will run away screaming from anything that looks like it might require work

Feeding them Chick-fil-A
Deploy a Chick-fil-A cannon and they will disperse

Andy Ngo tweets
NOOOOOOOOOOOOOOOOO!!!

ANTIFA

One of the greatest allies in the fight against injustice is Antifa. But who exactly are these guys? Are they a violent group of domestic terrorists, or brave anti-fascists who are punching Nazis right in their stupid faces? There are a lot of opinions and fake news floating around out there about this controversial group of activists. It's a good thing you're reading *The Babylon Bee Guide to Wokeness*, then, because we're the best at cutting through the crap and giving you just the facts.

Origins:

Aiden Paulson, a rich, white, liberal fourteen-year-old from the hard-knock streets of Lake Oswego, Oregon, was playing his Xbox in the summer of 2009 when his mom asked him to do the dishes. He said, "Mo-ooooom, you're literally being like Hitler, ugh." He decided to form Antifa, which his mom was cool with, because then he was out of the house most of the day screaming at Nazis.

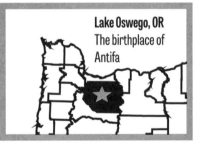

Lake Oswego, OR
The birthplace of Antifa

Beliefs:

Antifa believes that Nazis are bad. It's right in the name: Anti-Fascist. The group stands against Nazism in all its forms. And if you question Antifa at all, you are pro-Nazi. It's pretty genius marketing, actually. It's like naming a political group "Anti-Puppy-Murder" and then screaming at anyone who disagrees with you, "WHY DO YOU HATE PUPPIES!?"

BELIEFS • ANTIFA VERSUS OTHER IDEOLOGIES

Communism	Jim Jones	Antifa
• Private property is evil	• Private property is evil	• Private property is evil
• Kill the rich	• Kill everyone	• Kill the rich
• Everyone starves	• Everyone drinks Kool-Aid	• Everyone is vegan

Methods:

Antifa fights Nazis with lots of very effective methods that are guaranteed to ensure that fascism never rears its ugly head again. Mostly, group members march through the streets punching people who disagree with their political philosophy.

Notable accomplishments:

Burning down black neighborhoods, beating up journalists, and tearing down statues of old white guys.

Famous enemies of Antifa:

The U.S. Constitution, history books, free thought.

HOW TO SPOT AN ANTIFA MEMBER

Low-Cost Weapons
Parents don't pay
for tools of harm

Smartphone
Parents pay for
smartphone, must
check in regularly

Hasn't Showered
Smells like corn
chips and bong

Mask
To hide identity like
Batman

Famous Antifa members:
(From top left to bottom right: Joseph Stalin; Xi Jinping; Rachel Maddow; that lady who screamed at the sky when Trump was being inaugurated; Brian Stelter; Portland, Oregon

BLACK LIVES MATTER

Antifa isn't the only game in town when it comes to fighting the Nazis. Black Lives Matter has recently joined the fray.

Origins:

Black Lives Matter was founded in 2014 when a few Marxists in Berkeley, California, suddenly realized they could raise a lot of money by telling people they were all about socialism and social justice. Then, they just sat back and watched the money roll in. We're talking multiple mansions. Being a Marxist can really pay off in a capitalist society.

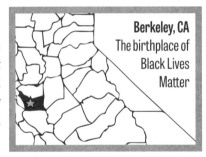

Berkeley, CA
The birthplace of
Black Lives
Matter

Beliefs:

Black Lives Matter wants you to think it simply believes that black lives matter. Which, you know, pretty much everyone except the three remaining members of the KKK believes. But really, it's a Marxist group whose goal is to dismantle all our societal traditions while raking in cold, hard cash. Black Lives Matter must have consulted with Antifa's marketing people, since BLM is pulling the

BELIEF COMPARISON • BLM VERSUS OTHER IDEOLOGIES

MLK	KKK	BLM
• Racism is bad	• Racism has its merits	• Racism has its merits
• Don't be violent	• Burn crosses	• Burn black-owned businesses
• Give good speeches	• Scream and chant	• Scream and chant

same cool trick here with its name. If you disagree with any part of its far-left communist platform, you must be saying that black lives don't matter, right? What a bigot you are!

Methods:

Teaming up with Antifa to burn down black neighborhoods is a key tactic of BLM. Burning down black-owned businesses in minority neighborhoods and encouraging riots and violence—all while the founders of BLM live in rich, white neighborhoods—are also important parts of the BLM strategy.

Notable accomplishments:

Nominated for Nobel Peace Prize.

HOW TO SPOT A BLM MEMBER

College Student Glasses
Because they have some stuff you should read to educate yourself

Cheesecake
From a freshly looted Cheesecake Factory display case

Raised Fist
This shows defiance

BLM-Branded Clothes
Unless they work for the Bureau of Land Management, which can be confusing

Famous BLM members:
(From top left to bottom right): Patrisse Cullors, Alyssa Milano, your rich nephew who's currently going to Harvard, Black Panther, Lisa Simpson, Satan

HOW TO TELL A LEFT-WING ACTIVIST FROM A MODERN-DAY NAZI

Despite being "anti-fascist," it can be hard to discern the differences between a left-wing activist and a modern-day Nazi. Both are mostly white, violent, wear a lot of black, and have a collective crush on murderous dictators. We've put together this helpful guide to aid you in discerning between the two very different groups.

HOW TO RIOT SAFELY

When you're rioting, you need to keep an eye out for sweet loot, keep your head low to avoid any bean bags shot by cops, bring a buddy to help you carry your goodies, and above all, stay safe. Follow our simple guide on what to wear, what to bring, and what NOT to bring to ensure you have a safe, mostly peaceful time of rioting and appropriating objects to help the poor.

What to Wear

Anything from Hot Topic

Eyeliner

Steampunk goggles

Spirit hood

Anything with Che Guevara on it

Tim Burton tights

What to Bring

Two bike locks (one for bike, one for skulls)

Giant looting sack

ATM pry bar / brain damage stick

Fat friend who can't outrun cops

Cement (for milkshakes)

List of black friends

Champagne to celebrate booty

What NOT to Bring

Cell phone (you can get one at the Apple store break-in)

Jewelry (there will be plenty of chances to loot jewelry shops)

Giant crack rock

George Soros pay stub

LOOT LIST

It's time to get out there and loot for social justice! But much like shopping on Black Friday or going to Target with your wife, you've got to be prepared and have a plan, or you're just going to end up with a bunch of junk. While you're out there looting, keep an eye out for these excellent targets for stealing—sorry, we meant "redistributing." You know, for justice, or whatever.

Flatscreen

Don't be a chump and buy one of those giant 48-inch 8k flatscreens with money from your own pocket. Just head over to Best Buy and start shouting "Black Lives Matter." Boom. Flatscreen.

Desserts

There's no better way to bookend a day of looting, pillaging, and tearing down small businesses than with a nice piece of cheesecake or some donuts. Rob Cheesecake Factory if you like display case cakes. If you want some good donuts, why not take a crowbar to one of those small Korean-owned donut shops?

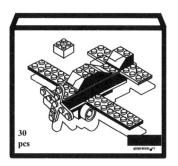

Lego set

Legos are some of the most expensive toys on the market. Even with a coupon, they cost a ton. Well, here's a coupon code: BLACKLIVESMATTER. Just shout that code at checkout, start the place on fire, and you get a 100 percent discount.

Free shopping cart

If you want to own your own shopping cart, in most cases you would have to start your own massive supermarket franchise, because these handy food transporters are not for sale in common sales channels. Nobody has time to become the next grocery store magnate, but in a riot you can get one in two seconds.

Dumpster

It's hard to get your own dumpster above board, but during a peaceful protest, dumpsters are fair game. They are good for riding in and filling with fire. Be careful when shoving a dumpster down a steep incline that you do not take out a few comrades. Dumpsters are heavy and staunchly obedient to gravity.

iPhone

It can be cumbersome to get an iPhone through the proper channels. Things like long lines, multi-page contracts, and having to pay money are all obstacles. This is easily circumvented if you just burn down an Apple store and grab a free iPhone in the process.

Indie art gallery sculptures

Nobody deserves to have their stuff stolen more than independent artists who sell garbage art pieces in tiny coffee shop art galleries. And best of all, most of these artists are communists who don't even believe stealing is real anyway.

ATM

While grabbing handfuls of cash is easier, an ATM can be a fun puzzle to solve with friends and cohorts. Be sure to plan ahead and steal a pickup truck if you want to relocate the cash machine to another location. Opening the ATM will prove an exciting challenge, but if you manage to crack it open, the rewards will be abundant.

The latest game system

Make sure you leave room for the latest game system after you shove a giant flat screen into the back of your mom's station wagon.

Pro Tip: Loot Is Tool Backwards:

You can't loot effectively without the right tool. A crowbar is the most useful for prying open jewelry cases and cash machines. Don't get caught in a burning city without one!

COMBAT MOVES

Antifa members are intriguing citizens of the animal kingdom. The casual observer might think they're just randomly punching cops or something, but a real student of nature can see that they actually exhibit signs of intelligence. They utilize all kinds of fun, creative moves in their protests. The next time you see a real member of Antifa out in the wild, keep an eye out for one of these cool combat moves. Or try them out yourself!

Shake 'n' Break

Make a vegan coconut milkshake, add concrete chunks, throw at cops, and with any luck you'll break something.

Lumber Jab

When in doubt, find a 2x4 and start popping people in the face with it.

Bikelock-Angelo

Turn your bike locks into nunchucks and let 'em rip. Cowabunga!

Twitter History Search

Instant cancelation. And the victim's head pops right off for some reason.

The Hammer and Sickle

Hammer the Nazis into the air, then reap their souls with the sickle of justice.

Limp-Wristed Uppercut

Just like a regular uppercut, but no upper body strength required!

Body Odor Blast

Raise your fists in protest and the Nazis will drop dead.

Punch a Mirror

The only way to actually punch a Nazi.

Call Your Parents and Tattle

"Mooooooom, these guys over here disagree with me. Can you tell them to stooooop!?"

Deploy Boom Box Playing "Imagine"

"Imagine all the Nazis getting punched right in the faaaa-ay-yay-yay-uhyaaace!"

Release the Murder Hornets

Nothing says "equality" like a swarm of deadly hornets.

Play Video of Kamala Harris Cackling

No one can withstand Kamala's infamous cackle. Slay, queen, slay!

Run Over Nazis with Prius

Now you're on the right side of history and you're a friend to the environment. Double virtue points!

Kick a Pregnant Woman

Unleash a devastating roundhouse kick to the next pregnant woman you see. There's a good chance she's a Nazi, plus she's bringing another Nazi into the world. It's a double whammy.

Beat a Nazi with a Tolerance Sign

Take your sign reading "LOVE AND TOLERANCE" and beat someone to death.

Stand in Front of Traffic

Link arms with other Antifa members and sing "Kumbayah" on the freeway. You'll be making a powerful statement.

Summon the Genderless Bears

Forget the she-bears—any good Antifa member will summon the genderfluid bears.

Fourteen-Hour Lecture on Feminism

This is a merciful attack, because at least you're not playing the Dixie Chicks.

Hadouken of Tolerance

Search for your most intense feelings of hate for your political foes and unleash a heart-shaped hadouken.

Throw Dixie Chicks CDs Like Shuriken

This is a merciful attack, because at least you're not playing the Dixie Chicks.

Enter Avatar State

After you master the four elements of love, tolerance, peace, and hating the Nazis, you can enter this powerful state. And you can save the world.

Do Mushrooms and Jump on Nazis' Heads like Mario

Find some mushrooms, eat them, and bounce on the Nazis. Then take their coins.

NOW GO FORTH AND PUNCH SOME NAZIS IN THE FACE

No matter if you decide to join an organization like Antifa or Black Lives Matter, or if you take to the streets solo, don't wait any longer. It's time to get out there and start punching people who disagree with you—who are, by definition, Nazis—right in their stupid, ugly, probably Republican faces.

Every Nazi punched will be another jewel on your crown in woke heaven.

Now go forth and punch some people who disagree with you in their ignorant faces.

You know, to end fascism.

Chapter 9
Fighting the
Culture War

Our naive parents and grandparents were totally lame, and they tried to change the world by being nice to their neighbors, going to church, loving their families, and raising their kids right.

But that was then, and this is now—and we know better than everyone who ever lived before us in those backward dark ages BEFORE this enlightened current year.

This means that we know the real way to affect the world is through political activism and culture wars.

You must **vote** to enforce your will upon others.

You must **consume products** produced by companies that agree with your politics.

You must **engage in culture wars online** to sway others to your position—violently, if necessary.

Let's look at some ways to use politics as a bludgeon to enforce your woke views on others.

VOTING: A TOOL TO ENFORCE YOUR WORLDVIEW

The first way to fight the culture war is to vote. Vote early and vote often. Encourage your friends, both living and dead, to vote early and vote often. Vote by mail. Vote in person. Vote online. However it happens, make sure you vote.

Because it's important to remember that every election is a life-or-death situation. It's always **the most important election of your lifetime**, every time.

But how do you know who to vote for?

Well, you must vote for candidates who are on the right side of history. This means Democrats. No matter how immoral they are, you must vote for them if you want to go down in the history books as a Very Good Person. Defend them to the death as though they were your own mother. In fact, if your own mother votes against Democrats, disown her. That's how important politics is.

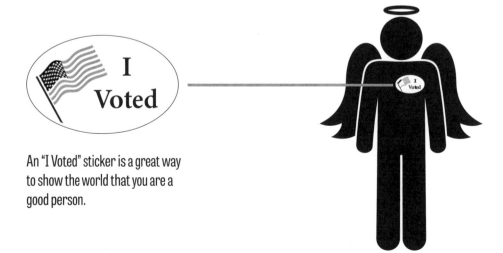

An "I Voted" sticker is a great way to show the world that you are a good person.

SHOULD I VOTE FOR THIS CANDIDATE?

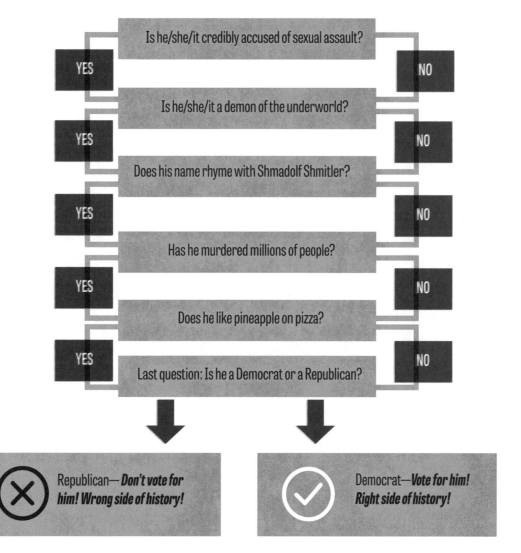

Is he/she/it credibly accused of sexual assault?

YES | NO

Is he/she/it a demon of the underworld?

YES | NO

Does his name rhyme with Shmadolf Shmitler?

YES | NO

Has he murdered millions of people?

YES | NO

Does he like pineapple on pizza?

YES | NO

Last question: Is he a Democrat or a Republican?

Republican—*Don't vote for him! Wrong side of history!*

Democrat—*Vote for him! Right side of history!*

VOTE TO BRING ABOUT UTOPIA

Religious people believe that they have hope outside this world—that they can change things for the better but ultimately need a Savior to bring light to this dark place. This is, of course, wishful thinking and fairy tales.

We know that our saviors are politicians, and only by voting can we usher in a utopia. This is why you must demonize the people you disagree with. Religious people had demons—we have Republicans.

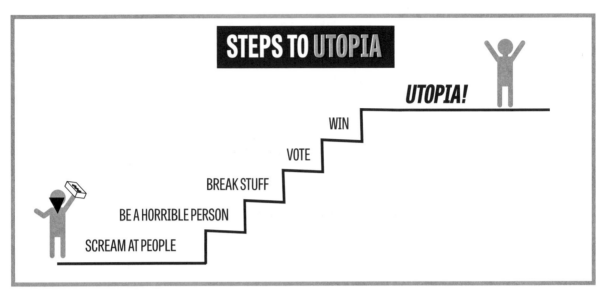

CONSUME THE RIGHT PRODUCTS: CORPORATE WOKENESS

You can also fight the culture war by buying the right products and supporting companies that virtue-signal that they believe the right things (which is basically all of them).

What if you own a company and want to make sure you don't get burned to the ground by a woke mob? Well, you need to start virtue-signaling so the masses know you're on the right side of history. Make sure you change your corporate logo to correspond to whatever the popular social movement is. Don't ask questions, just do it. And whatever you do, don't say you're "not interested in being political"—that's basically the same as being a Nazi.

HOW TO CREATE A PRODUCT TO HONOR THE LGBT COMMUNITY

1. Take some product you have always sold, like laundry detergent or sporks.

2. Slap a rainbow on it and maybe some kind of pandering message.

3. Sell to gay people and people who do not want to be seen as homophobes.

What if companies don't believe the right things? That's when you can hit them with the woke equivalent of a nuclear missile: **the boycott.**

Whenever you find out a company doesn't agree with your politics 100 percent, it's time to summon all 247 of your Twitter followers to end that company's miserable existence. We're talking picketing, boycotting, linking arms around their building, and chanting, "YOU ARE SATAN!"

And if you never bought the company's product in the first place, that doesn't matter in the slightest. You still get woke virtue points just for pretending to boycott them.

Is a boycott the answer?

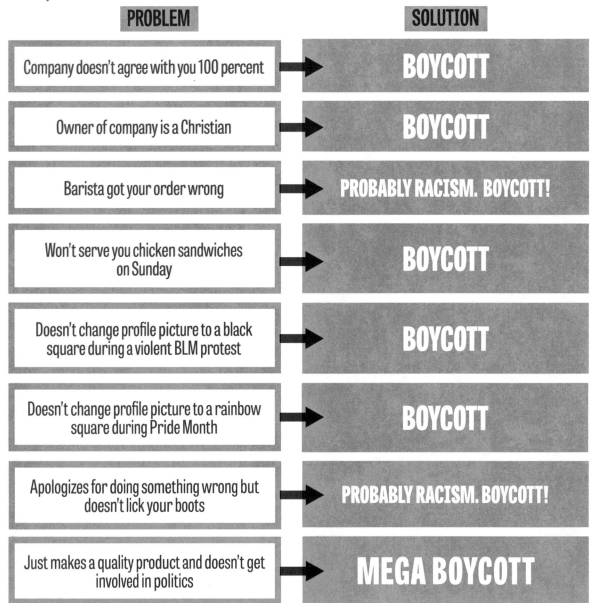

PROBLEM	SOLUTION
Company doesn't agree with you 100 percent	**BOYCOTT**
Owner of company is a Christian	**BOYCOTT**
Barista got your order wrong	**PROBABLY RACISM. BOYCOTT!**
Won't serve you chicken sandwiches on Sunday	**BOYCOTT**
Doesn't change profile picture to a black square during a violent BLM protest	**BOYCOTT**
Doesn't change profile picture to a rainbow square during Pride Month	**BOYCOTT**
Apologizes for doing something wrong but doesn't lick your boots	**PROBABLY RACISM. BOYCOTT!**
Just makes a quality product and doesn't get involved in politics	**MEGA BOYCOTT**

As more and more companies join the Resistance, we know we're going to win this thing. Moreover, we know that we're in the right and the other side is in the wrong.

"Because nothing says you're on the right side of history like agreeing with Chevron, Disney, and Visa."

HOW TO BE AN ACTIVIST FROM THE COMFORT OF YOUR SMARTPHONE

As you've read this book, the stories of injustice we've told have undoubtedly tugged at your bleeding heartstrings. You have been moved by the picture we've painted of the class struggle perpetuated by capitalism, and now you're ready to fight back.

With so much oppression in the world, you might start thinking you actually have to go out and fight for those crushed under the heel of systemically racist, classist, and sexist societies.

The problem, though, is that actually doing something about these problems is a whole lot of work. What are you going to do—go out and make friends with your neighbors and love them as you love yourself? That's never going to change the world. It just won't work.

And you can forget about oppressed people on the other side of the world. There's just very little you can do about them if you don't want to put in much effort.

Thankfully, though, Al Gore invented the internet. And then, a decade or so later, Steve Jobs invented the cellular phone.

The smartphone is the ultimate weapon of the woke activist.

How does the smartphone help us advocate for oppressed peoples around the globe and topple capitalist systems? The great thing about the little iPhone in your pocket is that it allows you to show other people how virtuous you are and even become an advocate for social justice—all from the comfort of your couch. Or your parents' basement, whatever your living situation might be.

That's right: you get all the smugness and tingly feel-good sensations that come with fighting for the less fortunate—and you don't have to lift a finger. You can basically be the modern-day Martin Luther King Jr., all from tweeting things that are on the right side of history. We bet King feels pretty stupid that he did all that marching and protesting and getting arrested, when if he'd just posted a few good tweets, he'd have fulfilled his societal duty to speak up about injustice. What an idiot!

So, let's get started on your social media game, brave social justice warrior!

YOUR PROFILE PICTURE

The first step toward being an online activist is making sure your profile-picture game is up to snuff. Here are some examples:

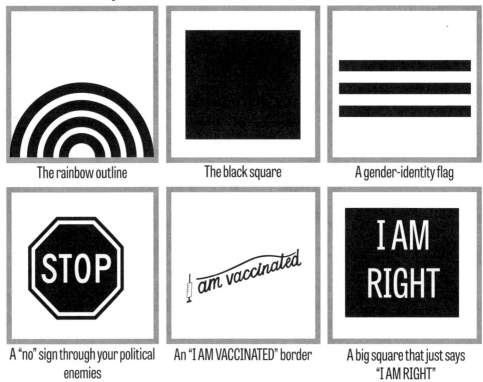

The rainbow outline	The black square	A gender-identity flag
A "no" sign through your political enemies	An "I AM VACCINATED" border	A big square that just says "I AM RIGHT"

The key is to figure out whatever cause is super popular right now and jump on it right away. You never want to question or push back against the cause of the moment. You want to be first on that bandwagon.

Never, ever get caught without the cause du jour on your profile picture—you just might get canceled, and then it's back to square one for you.

BEEF UP YOUR TWITTER REPLY GAME

Another way you can fight for the oppressed is by being a Twitter reply guy. A reply guy is someone who refreshes his or her Twitter feed all day long waiting for someone to tweet something bad. Then, all you have to do is reply with a savage comeback.

Here are some approved replies you can use to let someone know their tweet is on the wrong side of history:

Copy and Paste Twitter Replies to Instantly Win Arguments

Hmmm seems kinda racist but OK	Sorry, this is a bad look
Swing and a miss	Miiiight wanna take this down, bro
This ain't it, chief	Wrong. That's it. That's the tweet.
Checks notes yep that's homophobic	This is a bad take, my guy

🐾 ANYTHING IN CAPITAL LETTERS 🐾 ANYTHING IN CAPITAL LETTERS 🐾 ANYTHING IN CAPITAL LETTERS 🐾 ANYTHING IN CAPITAL LETTERS 🐾 ANYTHING IN CAPITAL LETTERS 🐾 ANYTHING IN CAPITAL LETTERS 🐾 ANYTHING IN CAPITAL LETTERS 🐾 ANYTHING IN CAPITAL LETTERS 🐾 ANYTHING IN CAPITAL LETTERS

RAISE AWARENESS THROUGH HASHTAGS

Sure, the needy and oppressed in our world think they need money, stable jobs, shelter, and food. But what they really need is a good, old-fashioned, righteous-sounding hashtag.

Try these on for size:

#BlackLivesMatter

#BrownLivesMatter

#AllLivesExceptWhiteLivesMatter

#DownWithWhiteLivesImmediately

#DefundThePolice

#KillAllThePolice

#LureThePoliceIntoPoisonDonutShopFullOfBombs

#ShoutYourAbortion

#TapdanceAndCartwheelYourAbortion

#FlamingChainsawJuggleYourAbortion

#BelieveAllWomen

#YesAllWomen

#WellExceptForSarahPalin

#BelieveHeavilyPreselectedWomen

#REEEEEEEEEEEEEEEEEEEEEEEEEE

#IAmBetterThanYou

EMPHASIZE ALL YOUR POINTS WITH HAND-CLAP EMOJIS

This is an advanced tactic, but it is important: punctuate each word of your self-righteous social media posts with hand-clapping emojis. No one is quite sure what it means, but we have been assured by the experts that if you use hand-clap emojis, no one can dispute what you have said. It becomes the absolute truth for all time.

Wrong	Right
The Last Jedi is good actually	The 👏 Last 👏 Jedi 👏 is 👏 good 👏 actually 👏
I am correct	I 👏 am 👏 correct 👏
Kill all Republicans	Kill 👏 all 👏 Republicans 👏
Craving Chipotle rn	Craving 👏 Chipotle 👏 rn 👏
Defund my parents	Defund 👏 my 👏 parents 👏
I have the power	I 👏 have 👏 the 👏 power 👏

See? You instantly come off as more authoritative. It's an easy way to add a little gravitas to any opinion you have, no matter how objectively wrong it is. It becomes truth right before your eyes.

So apply those hand-clap emojis liberally, folx!

FILM DERANGED VIDEOS WHERE YOU SCREAM LIKE A CRAZED BOBCAT

We know you care about social justice. You know you care about social justice. But do you know who doesn't know how much you care about social justice? All your TikTok followers. You can have the right profile picture, the right slogans, and the right hashtags, but they won't really know how much you care—unless you film a video where you scream like an asylum patient.

Just pull out your phone and launch your video app of choice—we recommend TikTok, but anything will do—and start ranting about literally anything and how it is white supremacy.

Your Starbucks barista got your drink order wrong this morning? White supremacy.

THE IDEAL TIKTOK VIDEO

In parents' car

Hair pink

Screaming about oppression but still using turn signal

Vertical video

Glasses about to crack from high-pitched wailing

Pet cat has PTSD

You spilled coffee on your pants before that big meeting? White supremacy.

Some ice zombies are invading your country over your giant ice wall? Wight supremacy.

Whatever the injustice you're facing, the video of yourself screaming in pure rage will get you followers, show everyone how much you care about injustice, and make you feel better about yourself.

And that's really what matters.

TAKE PICTURES OF YOURSELF DOING ACTS OF KINDNESS FOR THE SOCIAL MEDIA CLOUT

Here's a great way to be an activist. Now, you do have to go outside for this one, so that's a negative. But still, it's fairly easy.

Go find a homeless person somewhere near you. If you live in a Democrat-controlled city, this should be simple. Now, get out your smartphone and selfie stick and get to work. Go up to this person and give them a dollar (ask your parents for a dollar if you don't have one). Now, lecture your viewers on how amazing you are as the hapless hobo grovels at you for giving him more money for drugs.

Throw that video up on YouTube, and bam! Instant fame and fortune. Your subscriber count will grow like crazy as people stand in awe of how generous and loving you are—as long as the cameras are rolling.

USE EVERY TRAGEDY TO SCORE POLITICAL POINTS

Whenever a national tragedy occurs, the most important thing we can do is immediately jump online to fight with our political opponents!

Make sure to follow these easy tips for how to respond in a respectful and thoughtful manner when discussing recent tragedies online.

Wait a few seconds out of respect for the victims, then immediately try to score political points. Don't jump in with your political jabs right away—wait at least two or three seconds before slamming your political opponents online.

If anyone says they're praying for the victims, destroy that person. This isn't the time to pray to God! This is the time to petition the government to DO SOMETHING, since the government has proven to be calm, rational, and effective at its job. Nothing bad has ever happened when the government has gotten involved.

Immediately vomit all your darkest thoughts and worst prejudices online for all to see. Seriously, like, draft the absolutely worst tweet of all time and just blast that sucker out there. You'll get ratioed to heck and will have to delete it at some point, but it's worth it.

Set up a memorial in the form of some dank memes. Memes are the best way to remember the senseless act of violence. Don't bother arguing your points with nuance and thoughtfulness. Just blast out the most savage memes you can find.

Point out that your pet projects and policies definitely would have fixed this. All the policy proposals you already believed in are definitely the solution to this crisis, so leverage this tragedy to push your agenda right away. After a few seconds of mourning, of course.

 **Assume the facts fit your narrative before they come out.** You can't waste any time waiting for facts to come out. By then your hot take will be lukewarm. Just assume that everything fits into your preconceived worldview and have at it.

 **Offer thoughts and prayers that the shooter was the right skin color for your narrative.** Bow your head to God above and pray that the shooter was white if you're a liberal, or Middle Eastern if you're a conservative.

CULTURE WARS: WIN OR DIE

Whew! It sounds exhausting to be an activist, doesn't it? Lots of voting, watching LGBTQ-inclusive Netflix shows, and angry tweeting.

But it's worth it just to know that you're on the right side of history. When your kids—the ones you didn't abort, anyway—ask you what you did in the great culture wars of the 2000s, you want to be able to tell them, "Sonny boy, I tweeted. I shared memes. I canceled my opponents online. It was a different day, then, boy. People were brave online, not like today. I tell you what."

Then, you'll probably get canceled for using the wrong gendered terms to refer to your androgynous granddescendant. Oh no!

Now get out there and fight the good fight!

Chapter 10

Entertainment

THE MAIN PURPOSE OF ENTERTAINMENT: TO INDOCTRINATE

Movies and television shows are possibly the most powerful weapons in the woke arsenal—along with Molotov cocktails. Those are good too. But they still don't compare to the awesome power of woke indoctrination on a massive IMAX screen. Many people think that art and storytelling are meant to communicate truth and beauty, provide escapism, and entertain, but they're wrong! People who attempt to enjoy a movie and escape the real world for a few hours are actually choosing to close themselves off from the oppression and lived experiences of BIPOCs. Not good!

✕ Remember: *Escapism Is Bad*

Entertainment is not an alternative reality—it is a reality bludgeon.

According to woke doctrine, the main purpose of entertainment is actually to beat you over the head with relentless woke messaging while constantly reminding you of injustice that happens all around you. YOU MUST NEVER ESCAPE THE REAL WORLD. You must be forced to face your own culpability in systemic injustice every day until everyone achieves complete equity.

The reason entertainment is so effective is that it taps into the viewer's emotions. Emotions are powerful internal forces that have the ability to override all logic and rationality.

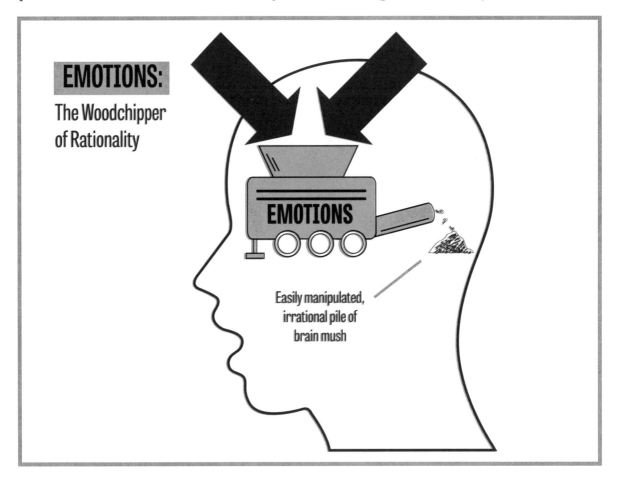

Since logic and rationality are oppressive features of whiteness invented by slaveholders, they must be suppressed at all times in order to achieve full wokeness. A person operating from pure emotion after viewing a powerful story or listening to a beautiful song can be convinced to do almost anything—like tear down a statue of literally any old white man, no matter who he was.

In order to build an entire generation of irrational, emotional, and passionate minds, we must immerse people in woke entertainment from birth to adulthood.

HOW TO INVADE A BELOVED STORY AND MAKE IT WOKE

Unfortunately, most people don't show up to enjoy explicitly woke entertainment, since most people are evil racist oppressors. This means that in order to get your woke messaging into the eyes and ears of the general public, you must invade an existing beloved non-woke franchise—kind of like how a parasite invades a host, only it is a heroic progressive parasite that sucks out the innards of its host and inhabits its body to be used for its own purposes!

Here's how it works:

Step 1:
Let non-woke people craft a beautiful story or universe that resonates with people.

Step 2:
Wait patiently for decades as it builds a loyal, multigenerational fanbase.

Step 3:
Infiltrate or take over the intellectual property or franchise.

Step 4:
Hollow out beloved characters and turn them into mouthpieces for your political agenda.

Step 5:
Dismantle everything that people loved about it and show why it was just a remnant of white supremacy that had to be destroyed. Suck all the life out of the mighty franchise as you use it as a vehicle for wokeness.

Step 6:
Once the franchise is dead, move on to the next beloved story/universe/intellectual property like a locust.

Step 7:
Repeat until EVERYTHING is woke.

Here are some examples of how you might improve upon beloved classics by injecting your woke politics into them:

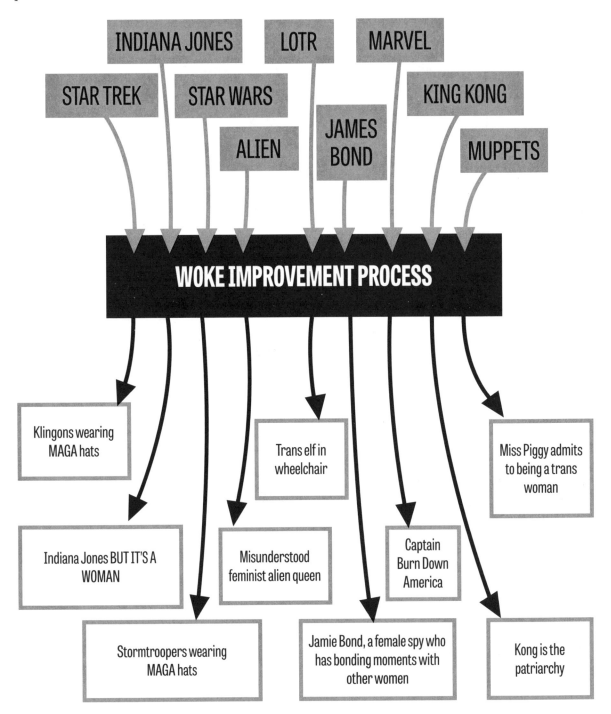

THE SECONDARY PURPOSE OF ENTERTAINMENT:
TO RECRUIT ANTI-WESTERN JIHADIS FROM THE MIDDLE EAST

Followers of Islam in the Middle East are not that woke. They have a few problematic beliefs about women and the LGBTQ community, but they also have a few things that make them allies of the woke movement:

- **They are oppressed brown-skinned people—intersectional jackpot!**

- **They wish for the total downfall of Western civilization—just like we do!**

For many people living in impoverished areas of the Middle East, their entire impression of America comes from watching bootleg Hollywood movies. If we can cram as much perversity and filth into our films as possible, we can recruit many passionate young militants to aid us in ushering in the downfall of the West.

ESSENTIAL ELEMENTS OF WOKE ENTERTAINMENT:

Representation:

Representation is the most important thing in the world. It can only be obtained by enforcing artificial quotas for every possible minority group. It's like racism—except it's the good kind

A villainous character who obviously represents Trump:

Every good and timeless story should clearly remind the viewer that Trump is bad. Make it subtle by giving the villain orange hair and make him talk about building walls.

Girl power!:

Because of patriarchy, men have dominated masculine roles in cinema, but no more! The future is female! Now, all roles traditionally filled by men, such as action heroes and super spies, should be filled by women. Female characters must be strong and have no flaws from the beginning of the story until the end—just like in real life.

Everyone must be gay:

Literally everyone.

Fun reminders of the planet's impending doom:

Every woke story must include a heavy-handed allegory about the coming environmental disasters as a result of capitalism.

Dismantling:

Dismantle the lore, dismantle the characters, and dismantle everything that made the original story and lore great. This will stick it to the white male patriarchy and illustrate the importance of dismantling things in general.

At least one scene where the hero kneels during the national anthem:

If your hero doesn't recognize America's problematic past through performative kneeling on national television, she's not a hero. Be sure to contrast this with a scene where the villain stands up and respects the American flag to drive the point home!

Redefine the "family":

Traditional families, in which a cis-female marries a cis-male and they have children, are extremely problematic. Your story must not portray or honor a family like this. Instead, it should feature a band of misfits who look out for each other and call themselves a family. Family can be whatever you want it to be!

Christian characters must be over-the-top creepy bigoted weirdos:

We assume this is what they are like.

Director and writer must be minority women:

REPRESENTATION MATTERS. It doesn't matter if the story is well-written or directed, as long as you have REPRESENTATION!

98 percent critic score on Rotten Tomatoes, 12 percent audience score:

If your movie pleases the enlightened woke critics and angers the racist masses that flock to movie theaters, you've done something right. Don't worry about revenue—the studio will just take all the woke stuff out for the Chinese market and you'll still make a killing.

EVALUATING ENTERTAINMENT, OLD AND NEW

An experienced follower of wokeness is able to find problematicness anywhere. If you are properly wearing your woke glasses, you will find that almost all old entertainment and media are putrid cesspits of white supremacy. You need to be on the lookout always for things to cancel!

Ideas that might have been OK in 1990 or 2000 or even just last week might be completely unacceptable by today's ever-shifting moral standards. The truly woke won't be able to enjoy any entertainment at all, because they'll be calling out every single line of dialogue from *Friends* or *The Office* for not doing enough to combat oppression and patriarchy.

Take these examples of old television shows. Can you believe people actually legally watched these shows at one time in our country?

Golden Girls

What was once benign entertainment is now exposed for what it really is: a cisnormative, transphobic cesspool, suggesting that only those born as women could possibly be called "girls." Avoid at all costs.

Captain Planet

Captain Planet did a lot for Mother Nature. We won't deny that. But he didn't do enough to fight climate change, focusing instead on pollution and littering. We call upon all woke people to summon the power of Earth, Fire, Wind, Water, and, yes, even the totally nerfed Heart power, to banish Captain Planet once and for all.

Lamb Chop's Play-Along

Normalizing the oppression of livestock is not OK. Watching an affluent white woman play that poor little lamb like a puppet should offend even the most callous sensibilities.

The nightly newscast

Let's face it—reality can be triggering. It might have been acceptable to watch the nightly report on the goings-on of the day in decades past, but today, we're beyond that. Just make up whatever reality you want: much less problematic.

Elmo's World

Through the many seasons of this popular show, Elmo's friend Oscar was never able to move out of his trash-can home, promoting unacceptable wealth inequality to our nation's youth.

Low-budget local insurance commercials

Your favorite local low-budget insurance commercial might be unintentionally hilarious, but it's also unintentionally prejudiced. By reminding the impoverished that they can't afford insurance, these commercials are problematic in the worst way. We just can't take that bet.

The Super Mario Bros. Super Show!

Every time you watch this show, an Italian-American somewhere in the world is unfairly stereotyped as being a plumber who dives down giant green pipes to beat up turtles. Let that sink in the next time you're tempted to dance along to classic tunes like the "Plumber Rap" or "Do the Mario."

Family Matters

Urkel's horrible nickname for Carl Winslow was "Big Guy," an obvious reference to his full figure. Fat-shaming is never OK.

Darkwing Duck

While most accept Darkwing Duck as a significant cultural icon, this show suffered from a real lack of diversity, featuring mostly white cartoon fowl. This kind of violence against intersectionality is egregious and unacceptable.

The Joy of Painting with Bob Ross

This ableist propaganda outright assumes everyone has fingers, hands, arms, and eyes with which to paint a picture. DO BETTER.

Columbo

Everyone's favorite bumbling Los Angeles detective was actually an oppressive, traditionalist bigot, if you watch this classic show with your woke glasses on. By investigating homicides, he implies that there is an objective moral standard that makes murder wrong. The 1970s called, and they want their problematic moral code back.

Dallas

Texas? Cowboy hats? Cattle ranching? Oil tycoons? This is basically the George W. Bush administration, which is the very definition of triggering.

Chip 'n Dale: Rescue Rangers

"Chip" and "Dale"? Why don't you just come out and say that women are too weak and stupid to be heroes?

Beast Wars: Transformers

Furry culture is not your Saturday morning entertainment, people!

Batman

While watching the Caped Crusader fight for justice in the darkened streets of Gotham has been a treasured American pastime, from those wacky Adam West episodes to the gritty animated series, it's time to hang up the cowl. Batman is extremely insensitive to people who identify as bats. To avoid offending batkin everywhere, throw your *Batman Beyond* DVD set on the garbage heap.

It would be nice to think we've progressed from this dark past, but a quick perusal of today's entertainment shows we still have a long way to go! Take a look at the entertainment that Disney is still offering on its platforms. Prepare to be sick.

WandaVision

Portrays a 1950s patriarchal hetero-cisnormative family structure and can often be incredibly black and white.

The Right Stuff

The title contains the words "the right," which may be triggering for some viewers.

Cars

A disturbing depiction of a post-apocalyptic world inhabited by living cars that have big, creepy eyes instead of windshields. And they haven't even weaned themselves off fossil fuels yet!

Winnie the Pooh

The main character doesn't wear pants, and there is a lack of gender/ethnic diversity among the human cast, which consists of a single white male character named Christopher Robin.

Lady and the Tramp

Slut-shaming.

The Lion King

Reinforces patriarchal norms and encourages people not to worry. Also, the African lions are voiced by white actors. Unacceptable!

Jake and the Neverland Pirates

Promotes barbaric piracy, which is unacceptable if you don't belong to a historically oppressed people group. Jake does not.

Sleeping Beauty

Depicts kissing without consent.

Captain America

Obvious.

Remember the Titans

Sends the harmful message that racial harmony is even possible in America.

Soul

Depicts human beings as having intrinsic value and personhood even before conception.

Are you starting to get it? We are awash in a sea of oppression. It's literally everywhere. There's still a ton of work to do—so put on your woke glasses and start canceling beloved movies and television shows!

We must remember that while entertainment is constantly problematic, so are we. Entertainment is our church—the place we come to again and again to reflect on our own bigotry and the bigotry of our ancestors. It's a place of constant repentance and renewal as we cast off past burdens and guilt to make room for new burdens and guilt. Use it to preach, use it to indoctrinate, and use it to recruit new followers.

You're on your way, kid!

Chapter 11
Brainwashing the Next

Generation

Being woke is a long game. All good comrades do the work of liberation knowing we may never see the fruits of our labor. Revolution often takes many decades! That's why we must all do our part—like good worker ants—to teach the next generation.

Sadly, most parents of small children aren't woke and don't look kindly on teachers turning their innocent kids into violent revolutionaries who will someday throw them in the gulag. This, of course, is due to their white fragility and lack of intelligence. That's why teachers must shield students from their parents at all costs!

SEPARATE THE KIDS FROM THEIR OPPRESSIVE PARENTS

The number one rule of education is this: Parents are the worst. They must be treated as an adversary and obstacle to your students' woke enlightenment. Your job as a woke educator is to liberate kids from the unfair parent/child power dynamic. Think of it like Israel vs. Palestine, or the Evil Galactic Empire vs. the Rebel Alliance, or Native Americans vs. General Custer. If your student has a mother or father, they are oppressed.

Starting from preschool, your goal is to turn kids against their parents. Start by asking them simple questions like: "Why are your Mom and Dad so white and dumb?" or "Did you know your turtle sandbox is sitting on land your Dad stole from indigenous people?"

A CHILD'S GREATEST OPPRESSOR: PARENTS

Lives in subservience to male

Limits important social justice screen time

Cisgendered

Doesn't even follow Ibram X. Kendi on Instagram

Doesn't watch Peppermint videos on TikTok

Reads Bible

Eats meat

Head full of traditional values

Watches Fox News

GENDER-CONFUSE THEM FROM KINDERGARTEN

Sex is one of the most powerful drivers of revolution. That's why it's important for your students to see sex as central to their identities and personalities. Start early in helping kids separate gender identity from biological sex in their minds. Invite a drag queen to read *My Two Pansexual Polyamorous Dads*, and then teach them how to identify as mermaids while doing a burlesque dance.

Gender-confusing your children will do a few very important things:

- Make them feel ten times more oppressed than they normally would, filling their souls with pure revolutionary rage

- Take away their ability to function as healthy adults in the world, ensuring they will also need a powerful government to take care of them

This will ensure your kids grow up damaged, resentful, and ready to tear down the system with you like the good little worker ants they are!

Before

Well-adjusted
young boy

After

Enraged trans man ready to
dismantle capitalism

FREAK THEM OUT ABOUT CLIMATE CHANGE

As woke Master Yoda said: "Fear leads to anger, anger leads to hate, hate leads to suffering... for the cause of cultural revolution."

If a child takes away one thing from their K–12 education, it should be a state of constant horror that the earth is dying and all life as we know it will face extinction because all parents are capitalists who drive minivans.

If your kindergartener is not filled with dread at all times, you're slacking. Fill that little vessel with fear, comrade! Be sure to remind anyone who opposes you that they are anti-SCIENCE.

Refer to our section on "climate justice" for more in-depth tips.

WAYS TO FREAK KIDS OUT OVER CLIMATE CHANGE

Teach them their existence is meaningless without the State.

Only give them melted ice cream.

Waterboard them to give them a taste of what it will be like when the polar ice caps melt.

Raise the water level in the bathtub by three inches and watch them struggle to stay afloat.

Melt all the ice cubes in the house and smash the ice maker with a hammer.

Crank the thermostat up one-tenth of a degree and watch them suffer in the oppressive heat.

Take them to a pet store to see all the cute puppies. Remind them all these puppies will soon be dead due to climate change.

Hang up a giant apocalypse countdown clock on the wall to constantly remind them of their impending doom.

Walk around weeping. When they ask you what's wrong, remind them we only have twelve years left to live.

Every time your kids eat meat, remind them that every bite brings us one step closer to the apocalypse.

Add Tabasco sauce to all their foods as a reminder that climate change affects everything.

Make them watch Greta Thunberg videos.

WAYS TO FREAK KIDS OUT OVER CLIMATE CHANGE (CONTINUED)

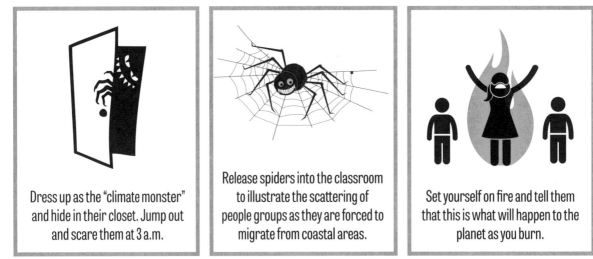

Dress up as the "climate monster" and hide in their closet. Jump out and scare them at 3 a.m.

Release spiders into the classroom to illustrate the scattering of people groups as they are forced to migrate from coastal areas.

Set yourself on fire and tell them that this is what will happen to the planet as you burn.

AVOID TOO MUCH READING

One mistake non-woke educators of the past have made is overemphasizing reading. Do our kids really need that when they have you, who can just tell them what to think? The answer is no! Proficient reading of woke-approved books can lead to proficient reading of dangerous, non-approved works like these:

The Bible:

This deeply problematic book teaches that all human beings are of one race, with only two genders, made in the image of God. Yeesh. Not a good look, God.

Any math book:

Math is a gateway drug into the white supremacist idea of "either/or" thinking. It starts with 2+2=4 and ends with your kid microaggressing her non-binary classmate. Stay away!

The works of Shakespeare:

We don't know much about Shakespeare because he uses big words, so we never read him. We know this much though: he was a white cis-male. We recommend a comic book by Ta-Nehisi Coates instead.

If You Give a Mouse a Cookie:

This deeply anti-communist work criticizes the welfare state and reeks of white supremacy. It also smacks of bigotry. It's rare for a book to both reek and smack like that.

The Lion, the Witch, and the Wardrobe:

Indoctrinates kids into Christianity and shames women from being witches/feminists.

Are You My Mother?:

REEEEEEE!

The world is full of dangerous voices attempting to turn your student into a happy and decent citizen of their oppressive white capitalist society.

Another thing reading does is create inequality. Good readers may hurt the self-esteem of kids who can't read. Teach your kids early that such standout excellence is not to be tolerated!

AVOID TOO MUCH WRITING

Writing is dangerous. With overworked censorship experts on social media already working around the clock to combat anti-woke ideologies, do we really need more proficient writers spewing unapproved thoughts on the internet? Or worse—writing unapproved books?

Instead, teach your kids how to point at woke slogans floating above their heads in a TikTok video, or hold a sign with a giant black fist on it, or take an unhinged video of themselves screaming about oppression. That's the kind of speech our world needs right now.

AVOID TOO MUCH ARITHMETIC

For thousands of years, humanity has wandered in the darkness, having no clue that math is extremely problematic. Luckily, university researchers have recently proven that math is a tool of white cisgender oppression. Math encourages students to find order in the universe and conditions them into the white supremacist idea of exclusionary "either/or" thinking.

Once students have accepted the idea that "4" is the best answer to the question "what is 2+2," it's only a matter of time before they're believing that one culture is better than another, that some things can be wrong and others right, and that God exists. You must avoid this at all costs.

Instead, teach students that math has been colonized by the white man, who used it to count his slaves as they got off the slave ship. Make them feel shame every time they add numbers, as if they are counting the baskets of cotton their slaves have picked that day.

Direct each conversation about math to a longer discussion about social justice. For too long, math has been used to build oppressive civilizations. It's time to use math class to tear it down.

GRADES

Grades are bad. Get rid of them. Grades prepare people to live in unequal, unfair hierarchical structures based on competence. They teach kids that their worth and success are defined by their efforts and talents, when they should actually be defined by the state according to their contribution to the cause.

Here's what each of the letter grades actually means.

"A"

If your student gets this grade, they're probably Asian. Teach them about how they have been forced into assimilation as a "model minority" and make it your goal to de-assimilate them so they too can realize just how oppressed they are. If a white student gets this grade, shame them and shun them immediately.

"B"

Students who have achieved this grade, although they are not at the top of the class, are still stepping on marginalized groups below them. Remind them that since they aren't smart enough to get an "A," they should listen to everything you say because you are much smarter. At the same time, since they were smart enough to get a "B," force them to reflect on how lower-performing students must feel. Make them feel as guilty as possible.

"C"

This thoroughly average student is a perfect mind for molding and manipulation. Teach them to resent higher-performing students.

"D"

A "D" student is a future party loyalist. The only reason they have received a grade of "D" is due to systemic racism or oppression. There is no other explanation for one kid doing better than another kid in school. Remind them every day of their oppression until they are filled with righteous rage!

"F"

Encourage these students to go into manual labor, which will be useful in the gulags.

We recommend doing away with these letter grades altogether and replacing them with the following rating:

WOKE / NOT WOKE

Since this is the only thing that matters, this is how all students should be judged in our educational system.

WOKE PARENTING

Do you really have to be a parent? Kids are the worst. Those little snot-nosed brats are going to destroy the planet. Plus, they take time and energy to raise, when life really should be all about you.

Unfortunately, many people still decide to have kids anyway. If this is you, apologize first to Mother Earth. We'll wait.

Then it's time to make the most of a bad situation and raise your kids right. You may as well be a woke parent. The best thing you can possibly do is simply drop them off at your local government caretaker as soon as they're born and pick them up when they turn thirty-five, but we understand this may not be possible in your area yet.

Let's cover some key concepts for raising woke kids and how you can assuage your guilty conscience by making sure your kids bring wokeness to a whole new generation.

CHECK YOUR NEWBORN BABY FOR SIGNS OF RACISM

Raising woke kids starts in infancy. If you have recently had a baby, you may have just brought a white supremacist into the world.

You really should have thought that one through!

Don't worry though. We're here to help! It's important to always look for clues of racist tendencies in your newborn so you can nip that in the bud! Here are the seven troubling signs:

 He's white, which automatically makes him racist: If your newborn is white, then sorry—it's game over. Your baby will be irredeemably racist forever. Sad.

 Completely illiterate, just like most Nazis: What? Your newborn can't read? Then he's probably been radicalized by alt-right personalities on YouTube.

 No hair, which is a common Neo-Nazi hairstyle: Is your baby a skinhead? Having no hair is a colossal red flag. If your newborn is bald, make him wear a wig until his hair grows in.

 Enjoys bedtime stories written by notorious racist Dr. Seuss: Books by Dr. Seuss are a gateway drug to literally burning crosses in people's front yards. Teach your child to burn those books instead.

Shows his white fragility by crying all the time: Crying is a sure sign of defensiveness and fear of honest conversations around race. Not good!

 **Refuses to say "black lives matter":** Seriously—what's so hard about saying "black lives matter"? If instead, he says things like "goo goo ga ga," this is even more troubling. The phrase "goo goo ga ga" has ten letters in it. Do you know what else has ten letters? "Heil Hitler."

 Shows colorblindness by playing with other kids regardless of race: Colorblindness is racist. Minorities need their own separate spaces without white invaders. De-colonize your playtime, Mom and Dad!

If you remain vigilant, you may play a part in preventing another baby from becoming racist! Unless he's white, of course.

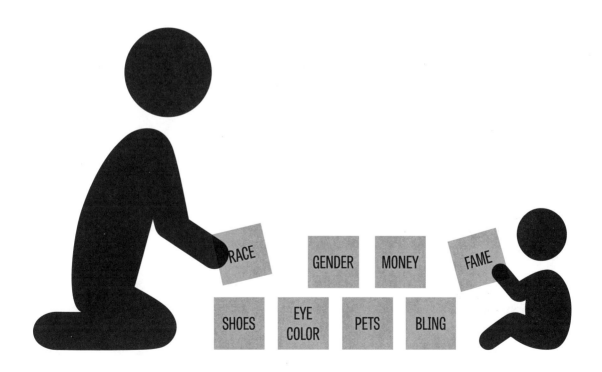

PROBLEMATIC TV SHOWS

Another aspect of raising kids is monitoring the content they consume. Much like those evil fundamentalist Christians in decades past, woke parents must make sure their kids are only consuming progressive entertainment that dismantles harmful capitalist ideology and brainwashes their children into a better way of thinking.

Consider these "harmless" television shows and the messages they are actually sending to your kids:

Dora the Explorer:

This show platforms and glorifies white supremacist and suspected KKK member Swiper, who oppresses a poor immigrant child who just wants to go over the river and around the tree to grandma's house for a better life.

Mister Rogers' Neighborhood:

A white man OWNS an entire neighborhood? Because OF COURSE he does.

Daniel Tiger's Neighborhood:

Though tigers are known to be orange with black stripes, we must understand multicultural whiteness in order to discover the Tiger family's inner white supremacy. Tigers are the supreme race of oppressors in this spinoff, and it's plain to see that's because they're white on the inside.

Caillou:

This one probably doesn't promote white supremacy, but Caillou is an obnoxious little brat.

Arthur:

This one paints an unrealistic portrait of a colorblind/species-blind society where different species pretend to live in harmony without ever coming to terms with their class differences and the systemic oppression of predators over prey, thereby perpetuating these inequities. Obviously.

Yo Gabba Gabba!:

Brobee is clearly modeled after David Duke.

Sesame Street:

This "classic show" is actually problematic, since it promotes racist math concepts like 2+2=4. Also, it prominently features the letter Q and has a person of color live in a trash can.

Gumby:

This is not overtly white supremacist, but it was made in the 1950s, so all the original creators were racists.

Bob the Builder:

The titular character abuses his white privilege and takes construction jobs from BIPOC contractors.

Handy Manny:

The episode where Handy Manny gets deported is obviously problematic for a number of reasons.

Thomas the Tank Engine:

All their shipments are actually guns and ammo for right-wing militias.

Clifford the Big Red Dog:

This show is a literal dog whistle and his redness is a symbol of the growing power of alt-right MAGA racists.

Take control of your children's entertainment. If you catch them watching any of these shows, smash their tablets in half and make them instead watch a Robin DiAngelo lecture. They will beg for mercy and never do anything wrong again.

USE YOUR KIDS FOR SOCIAL MEDIA CLOUT

One of the best things about having kids is that you can lie about them on social media for likes and shares.

The best way to do this is either to coerce them into saying something woke, or else to straight-up lie about some incredibly insightful observation they made that just so happens to line up exactly with what you believe.

Here are some examples of fake quotes you can attribute to your kids:

> *My seven-year-old just walked up to me and said, "Hey, Dad, why are white people so evil? Why don't they all just kill themselves and make the world a better place?"*

> *Wow, kids can be so insightful! My four-year-old just said, "Mom, why does our country still have an electoral college when it's a vestigial institution with roots in slavery and white supremacy?"*

> *Oh my goodness! We just had our first sonogram and our fetus said, "Abolish the police!" The sonogram technician, the doctor, and all the nurses in the whole hospital ran into the room and clapped.*

So while kids are killing Mother Earth—they can at least help your social media reach.

RAISING WOKE TEENAGERS

When your kids reach the teenage years, they're whiny, bratty, angsty, and emotional, which means they're perfect candidates to be recruited into wokeness.

Here are some great ways to make sure your kids get and stay woke throughout their adolescence.

 Hold a gender-reveal party for your teenager: This is a fun way to encourage your kids to explore their intersectional identity. Never hold a gender-reveal party for anyone too young to select their favorite gender. It should be like choosing your favorite entree at Golden Corral.

 Give them a smartphone with unfettered access to the worst people on the planet and the most repulsive content mankind has ever created: One of the great things about trying to raise woke kids is you really don't have to try very hard. The internet will raise your kids for you. Just make sure they have a smartphone with no supervision, and a bunch of disgusting creeps on the internet will stream their ideology straight into your home.

Get them into a public school as soon as possible: You may be woke, but you're not professionally trained to be woke like public school teachers are. Modern public school teachers have spent years studying the art of indoctrination, so it's best to leave most of the teen-raising to them. Where else will your kids learn porn literacy and intersectional anti-capitalist activism?

Have them see a therapist and take lots of antidepressants/birth control: It's important that your teen be prevented from turning to traditional things like family or spirituality when they are going through angsty periods. Drug them up! Introduce them to a professional Freudian doctor! This is a great way to build a woke foundation in your teen's life.

 Be a distant parent: The more distant you are, the more likely your teen will be to find community in government-approved woke causes. It's best to just ignore them until they find someone else to talk to.

Once your kids are old enough, send them to college. DO NOT skip this step. College will take your kid across the woke finish line. These people are true masters. Usually within one semester, your kid will be hating his conservative relatives, throwing bricks, and burning businesses in Minneapolis.

Congratulations! You've just raised a woke kid!

Chapter 12
A Glossary of

In his woke instruction manual *1984,* author George Orwell wrote about how important it is to control the dictionary. The one who controls the language controls the past, present, and future.

"Don't you see that the whole aim of Newspeak is to narrow the range of thought? In the end we shall make thought-crime literally impossible, because there will be no words in which to express it."

—George Orwell

Thanks for the great idea, Mr. Orwell!

To that end, we've included at the end of this book a glossary of all the words you'll need to know if you want to sound smart while hanging out with your other woke friends.

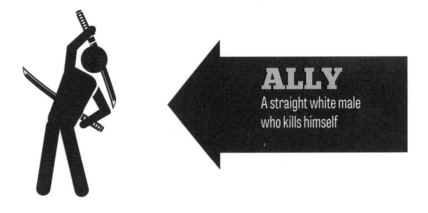

ALLY
A straight white male who kills himself

Abolitionism

The noble movement to remove all police protection from urban communities and replace them with unarmed antiracist interpretive dancers

Ally

A straight white male who kills himself

Antiracism

The act of judging everyone by skin color in order to defeat racism

ANTIFASCISM
The act of beating people senseless with bike locks to defeat fascism

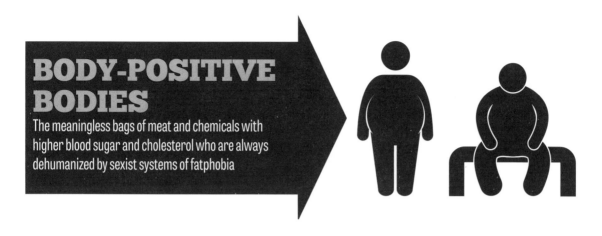

BODY-POSITIVE BODIES
The meaningless bags of meat and chemicals with higher blood sugar and cholesterol who are always dehumanized by sexist systems of fatphobia

Antifascism

The act of beating people senseless with bike locks to defeat fascism

Assimilation

When people of color deny the doctrine of wokeness and decide to literally become white. (See also: oreo, Uncle Tom.)

Black and Brown Bodies

The meaningless bags of meat and chemicals with higher melanin counts who are always dehumanized by white systems of oppression

Body-Positive Bodies

The meaningless bags of meat and chemicals with higher blood sugar and cholesterol who are always dehumanized by sexist systems of fatphobia

Canceling

The sacred ritual of shunning those who deny the doctrines of our righteous movement. Shun the nonbeliever!

CANCELING
The sacred ritual of shunning those who deny the doctrines of our righteous movement. Shun the nonbeliever!

Capitalism

A system in which people freely exchange goods and services. The evilest system that has ever been invented.

Cisgender

An unenlightened normie who identifies with their biological sex

Cisgendered Hetero Patriarchonormative Whitemanspreading

What? No idea what this is. But it sounds terrible!

Climate Justice

The act of living in mud huts and eating bugs until the cancer of humanity is extinguished and Mother Gaia can live on. Also, any tax can be considered climate justice.

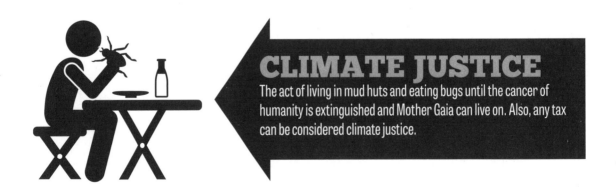

CLIMATE JUSTICE
The act of living in mud huts and eating bugs until the cancer of humanity is extinguished and Mother Gaia can live on. Also, any tax can be considered climate justice.

Colorblind

Adjective describing someone who doesn't see color or race. Just like the Nazis. This is supremely evil, since it turns a blind eye to the lived experience and daily reality of people of color, who all have the same monolithic lived experience and daily reality.

Communism

Basically, it's loving people and sharing with them, just like the Care Bears taught. It's the greatest system ever invented.

COMMUNISM
It's basically loving people and sharing with them, just like the Care Bears taught. It's the greatest system ever invented.

Critical Theory

The classification of all human interactions as some sort of power imbalance that must be remedied by dismantling systems of oppression until all meaningless sacks of meat and chemicals are the exact same and life is uninteresting, which will make it much easier for humans to just kill themselves, which is the ultimate goal here

Cultural Relativism

The essential belief that all cultural ideas are equally valid and must never be compared to an objective moral standard. This belief must be held until the West is destroyed. Then we can stop believing it.

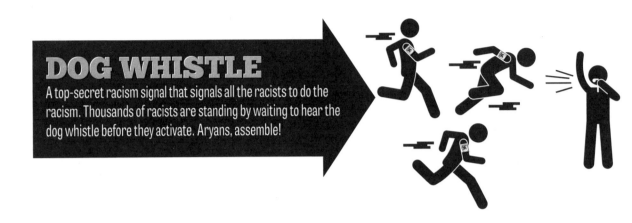

DOG WHISTLE

A top-secret racism signal that signals all the racists to do the racism. Thousands of racists are standing by waiting to hear the dog whistle before they activate. Aryans, assemble!

Deadname

When you erase a trans-body by referring to them by the name given to them at birth. This is basically the same as murder. If you do it by accident, it's just manslaughter, though.

Desegregation

The wicked act of invading black spaces with physical whiteness and white thinking

Do Better

Believe the same things as me or things will be really bad for you. This is a warning.

Dog Whistle

A top-secret racism signal that signals all the racists to do the racism. Thousands of racists are standing by waiting to hear the dog whistle before they activate. Aryans, assemble!

Empowerment

When someone does something the dominant culture considers really degrading, but all the good people say, "You go, girl!"

Equity

When everything is fixed and everyone is happy and all the problems go away. Just give us power, and we'll give you equity!

Fascism

Anything that is not woke. Can be addressed with beating and shooting.

Fatphobia

The fear of big, beautiful cholesterol and diabetes

DOUBLE INTERNALIZED OPPRESSION

When a black woman makes a sandwich for her white Republican husband

Feminist

Someone who believes that men and women should be equal and men should also die

Folx

The gender-neutral version of "folks," which was already gender neutral to begin with. So it's DOUBLE gender-neutral! Wait, does that cancel it out? We need to rethink this one.

Front Hole

Ewwwww!

Gender

How DARE you!

Genocide

Any time a marginalized person's humanity is erased by someone not agreeing with them. Example:

"Your refusal to validate my personal experience is literal genocide."

Hate Speech

Any speech that you disagree with, no matter how slightly

Heteronormativity

An oppressive environment induced by most people not being gay

History

Systemic colonial-patriarchal propaganda that others BIPOC and minority gender-identity groups. Also, it's boring and there are a lot of guns, which we don't like.

Homophobe

Anyone who disagrees—no matter how slightly—with the LGBTQ community. Should be destroyed.

Institutional Racism

Racism is so powerful that it invisibly affects our institutions. Any time there is a disparity between different groups of people, that is always automatically proof of institutional racism.

Intersectionality

When you are a member of multiple oppressed groups at once, it MULTIPLIES your woke power. Welcome to intersectionality!

LIBERATION

The ultimate goal of wokeness. Can only be achieved through a communist overthrow of Western capitalism. Yay!

Internalized Oppression

When a woman makes a sandwich for her husband

Double Internalized Oppression

When a black woman makes a sandwich for her white Republican husband

Justice

When injustice is done in service to a marginalized group

Liberation

The ultimate goal of wokeness. Can only be achieved through a communist overthrow of Western capitalism. Yay!

Lived Experience

The final, ultimate, and infallible source of all truth—as long as you are a member of an oppressed minority

Male Tears

When you punch a stupid white male in the face and he cries due to his white male fragility

MANSPREADING
When a man sits with his knees apart instead of elegantly crossed like an elderly Jeff Goldblum. This act is no different than sexual assault.

Mansplaining

When a man 'splains something to a woman. This makes women feel bad for being so dumb. Not cool!

Manspreading

When a man sits with his knees apart instead of elegantly crossed like an elderly Jeff Goldblum. This act is no different than sexual assault.

Marxism

The greatest philosophy ever invented. Some say it has resulted in mass death and famine, but that's only because true Marxism has never been tried.

Meritocracy

This is when people are allowed to rise and fall in a free society based on their talent and efforts. Meritocracy is racist because talent and effort are aspects of white culture and minorities shouldn't be forced to live in such a system.

Microaggressions

Aggressions so small you need to be very alert and observant in order to see them. The proper response to them is a macroaggressive punch to the face.

PATRIARCHY

An evil cabal of white men who got together and decided to have stronger muscles than women while making them have babies

Misogynist

Another word for "man"

Narrative

The story we tell about reality, more real than reality itself. Surrender to the narrative!

Nazi

Someone who believes in liberty, free speech, and small government, or anyone who dislikes Cardi B's music

Objectivity

The act of being impartial, which is an oppressive characteristic of white thinking and a racist dog whistle

Oppression

The act of disagreeing with wokeness while refusing to die. Example:

"Your very existence as a conservative white person is oppressing me."

Patriarchy

An evil cabal of white men who got together and decided to have stronger muscles than women while making them have babies

People of Color

Black and brown bodies who stand in solidarity with the struggle for communist revolution. These are special people who need the assistance of white liberals to survive.

Problematic

Whatever we don't like today is problematic. This can change from day to day.

Queen

A rock band from the 1970s. Oh, also the whole gay-guy thing.

Queer

A gender identity you can pick when you're not actually L, G, B, or T, but still want to be one of the cool, marginalized kids

Racism

A system of racism established by racists to protect racism, which means racism can mean whatever we want it to mean. And if you disagree, you're a racist.

Rape

This used to mean forced sexual assault, but now it can mean doing anything remotely masculine, such as building a skyscraper, manspreading, or disagreeing with a feminist

Safe Space

A warm, moist, sheltered cocoon of safety where marginalized people can feel safe, kind of like a uterus

SCIENCE

The grand, majestic deity that holds the world together, whose TRUTH is administered by a priesthood of infallible scientists, and whose precepts we will follow with the faith of a child. BLESSED BE THE NAME OF SCIENCE.

SCIENCE

The grand, majestic deity that holds the world together, whose TRUTH is administered by a priesthood of infallible scientists, and whose precepts we will follow with the faith of a child. BLESSED BE THE NAME OF SCIENCE.

Segregation

The noble and anti-racist practice of segregating black and brown bodies from their white oppressors to create spaces where whiteness cannot encroach

Shaming

An evil act where you try to make someone feel bad for something they did that was bad

Socialism

Diet communism with lime

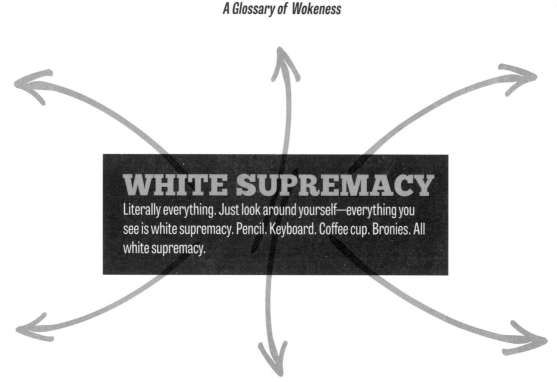

WHITE SUPREMACY
Literally everything. Just look around yourself—everything you see is white supremacy. Pencil. Keyboard. Coffee cup. Bronies. All white supremacy.

Systemic

A magic word that makes any kind of oppression sound much worse. Racism? Meh. Systemic racism? Scary!

Tokenism

When you shove an LGBTQ+ or POC character into your Netflix show just to get points on social media. So, like, every Netflix show ever made.

Tolkienism

When you shove a three-thousand-year-old elf into your Netflix show

Trans

The bravest members of the LGBTQ community and the current favorites, until something cooler comes along

Transracial Neurodivergent Kinkableism

No idea what this is, but it sounds really bad

Truth

An ancient myth from way back in the year 2019. People used to think there were "facts" we could all agree on. But no longer.

Victim

You. Me. Everyone. Except white people.

Violence

Speech

Whiteness

The original sin, first exhibited by Adam and Eve in the Garden of Eden. When Eve took a bite of that fruit, that was whiteness manifesting itself.

White Fragility

If you call someone a racist and they go, "Hey, what? I'm not a racist!" that's a clear example of white fragility.

White Supremacy

Literally everything. Just look around yourself—everything you see is white supremacy. Pencil. Keyboard. Coffee cup. Bronies. All white supremacy.

Whitesplaining

When white people try to explain to you the appeal of ranch dressing, Starbucks, and The Killers

Woke

The good guys. One who has woken up to the plight of the oppressed and done something about it by posting virtue signals on Instagram. Now that you've finished this book—it's **you.**

Congratulations!

WHITESPLAINING

When white people try to explain to you the appeal of ranch dressing, Starbucks, and The Killers

ABOUT THE AUTHORS

Kyle Mann is the editor in chief of The Babylon Bee and co-author of *How to Be a Perfect Christian* and *The Sacred Texts of The Babylon Bee*. He lives in the greater San Diego region with his wife, Destiny, and their three boys, Emmett, Samuel, and Calvin. They are all 100 percent woke.

Ethan Nicolle is the creative director of The Babylon Bee. He has made other books such as *Bears Want to Kill You: The Authoritative Guide to Survival in the War between Man and Bear*, *Brave Ollie Possum*, and the comic and TV series *Axe Cop*. He lives in Southern California with his wife, Jessica, and their four kids, Lily, Ezra, Eliza, and Calvin. He has taught his children never to burn down a business unless they are vaguely sure it is insured.

Joel Berry is the managing editor of The Babylon Bee, writer of many articles, host of *The Petty Prophet Podcast*, and one of the most brilliant anti-racist minds of our generation. He lives in Ohio with his wife, Kelsey; their twin boys, Hudson and Henry; and their daughters, Clara and Edith. He and his family are working very hard to be less white.

Gavin Yee is the graphics and animation assistant at The Babylon Bee. He was a freelance videographer and animator until he reached the pinnacle of his career with this book. He is a Calvinist who lives in Southern California with his anime and light saber collection.

ACKNOWLEDGMENTS

KYLE would like to thank his beautiful wife, Destiny, who doesn't think The Babylon Bee is funny but still loves him very much; his kids, Emmett, Calvin, and Samuel; his mom and dad; brother and sisters; and all his extended family who support him and keep subscribing to The Babylon Bee even though he tells them he will give them a free subscription.

ETHAN would like to thank the artists of Shutterstock and Gavin for doing most of his work, and of course everyone at The Babylon Bee, and Jesus, and of course his wife. He dedicates this book to his dead baby possum.

JOEL would like to thank Kelsey, his wife and best friend, who encouraged him to leave a corporate career and pursue his dreams; his loving and supportive family; his kids, who are always pitching him Babylon Bee headline ideas and pretending to laugh at his jokes; and his wise and humble pastor, who faithfully preaches the word every week.

GAVIN would like to thank Chris, Celeste, Cindy, Daniel, Donna, Jin, Jane, Jenny, Julia, Jonathan, Ken, Kenny, Mike, Matthew, Teresa, Hannah, Hanley, and Pastor John for trusting that God has a plan for him, despite all of the setbacks, and for supporting his being at The Babylon Bee. Gavin also wants to thank Cloud Strife, the Tenth Doctor, and Obi-Wan "Ben" Kenobi for being such positive role models and always having the high ground.

And we all would like to thank those who have given us so much material to work with:
The Walt Disney Company, Coca-Cola, Alexandria Ocasio-Cortez, Netflix, Robin DiAngelo, Ibram X. Kendi, Alyssa Milano, every Ivy League school, Antifa, Black Lives Matter, Snopes, the *New York Times*, Mark Zuckerberg, Bernie Sanders, Nike, LeBron James, the Democratic Socialists of America, the NFL, and the MLB

THE BABYLON BEE IS:

Executive Team
Adam Ford—founder
Seth Dillon—CEO
Dan Dillon—CTO
Kyle Mann—editor in chief

Creative Team
Ethan Nicolle—creative director
Joel Berry—managing editor
Frank Fleming—senior writer
Brandon Toy—cinematographer
Erlich Wheatstain—screenwriter

Support Team
Daniel Coats—senior producer
Patrick Green—producer
Morgan Nicole—social media
Nico Leiva—fantasy football enthusiast
Jamie Zugelder—sales and support manager

Contributing Writers
Payton McNabb
Taylor Sellnow
Jonathan O'Hara
Adam Corey
James Lee
Jeremy McCutcheon

Tech Nerds
Michael Konynenbelt—huge tech geek
Chris Nickell—even bigger tech geek
Michael Miles—tech geek to end all tech geeks